Hankie Couture®

HANDCRAFTED FASHIONS FROM VINTAGE HANDKERCHIEFS

Marsha Greenberg

RUNNING PRESS
PHILADELPHIA · LONDON

Printed in China

9 8 7 6 5 4 3 2 1

Digit on the right indicates the number of this printing

Library of Congress Control Number: 2010933196

ISBN 978-0-7624-4017-7

Photo styling and line drawings by Joy Chu
Photographs by Bryan E. McCay
Edited by Barbara Clark and Cindy De La Hoz
Cover designed by Corinda Cook
Interior designed by Joy Chu
Typography: Bernhard Modern, Helvetica Neue, Times, and Wendy

Running Press Book Publishers
2300 Chestnut Street
Philadelphia, PA 19103-4371

Visit us on the web!
www.runningpress.com

This book is dedicated to my mom,
who first taught me how to sew.
Mom, you were the best mom
in the world, the universe,
the galaxy, and the stratosphere!
I love you forever.

Contents

THE STORY OF

Hankie Couture®

I have always had a love affair with fabric.

As far back as I can remember, I was attracted to patterns and color. Since 2002, I have designed and sewn several thousand one-of-a-kind vintage handkerchief dresses . . . and I see no end in sight! The passion comes alive every day when I wake up. Sometimes I surprise even myself!

I love, love, love creating, designing, and sewing. The ideas just keep on coming, even in my sleep! One time, I had this amazing dream. I was having a problem with a doll hat. I could not figure out the best way to make the pattern. That night, in my dream, the solution was placed in my head. I woke up about 4:00 a.m. (an hour earlier than I usually awaken), got out of bed, went downstairs, made the pattern, sat down and sewed it, and it worked! Wow!

As a ten-year-old, I was already toying with doll clothes. I used to make dress patterns out of old newspapers, then cut out my amateur creation and fit it to my doll. My mom bought me this tiny little Singer sewing machine. It was a very well-made, heavy machine from London. (I still have it!) There was a wheel on the side that you turned to make the needle go up and down and I would sit for hours sewing the day away.

The only formal training I've ever had took place when I was eleven years old and my mom enrolled me in a summer sewing course. The class assignment was to choose a simple style . . . nothing too difficult, lest we become discouraged! Everyone in the class chose garments without sleeves, collars, zippers, or pleats. I chose a dress with a twenty-two-inch zipper, set-in sleeves, an inverted pleat, a dropped waist, a collar, neck facings, and long, long darts. Even then I could not follow the path of least resistance! My

thought process was: If I'm going to invest my time in something, it better be spectacular.

Not too long after that, I started making my own clothing. By the time I was in junior high, I had made so many dresses for myself that I could go thirty days without repeating an outfit.

I have my mom to thank for teaching me to squeeze the most out of any piece of fabric. Many times I was short on the amount I needed by a half a yard or more. Together we would ponder the placement of the pattern pieces and manipulate them to fit. We were always successful. Eventually I learned to make my own patterns. Many years later I even took a course in formal pattern drafting, but I found it tedious. So I went back to my own methods.

As a young teenager, I taught myself every craft you can imagine: knitting, crochet, embroidery, cross-stitch, needlepoint, beading, and smocking, to name a few. When my friends would be hitting the trendy fashion stores, I would pay a visit to the fabric store. I loved the feel of fabrics and I loved all the different patterns.

Fast forward to my own business of designing and manufacturing women's clothing for a company called Marsha, Inc., which I founded in 1978 with my husband, Brian. We started with a simple wrap skirt and then added other styles, including a reversible version as well as matching tops, pants, and jackets. I was in my element, a dream come true for a fabric junkie!

Every season (there are five in the garment industry—spring, summer, fall, winter, and holiday), fabric reps would come to the factory and "romance" the new line. I saw thousands of swatches and I always picked the best. All the buyers said the same thing: "Marsha, you sure have an eye for prints!"

After we sold our business in 1986, I began designing custom-made dresses for private clients. In the course of my travels, I always made sure to stop at the local fabric store. Naturally, I carried my purchases home with me on the airplane. I did not trust my fabric gems to the luggage compartment! No way! And once home, I didn't cut them up immediately. Instead, I looked at them for a long time and contemplated the designs. In time, the right style came to me. Now, I never go anywhere without my tape measure, paper, and pencil. I never know when or where I'll see something that triggers a thoughtful idea.

ABOVE: Here I am at age eleven—already an aspiring clothes designer.

LEFT AND BELOW: My very first sewing machine, along with its original box. I spent umpteen hours at this little machine!

One day in 2002, I was on an antiquing trip to Adamstown, Pennsylvania (Brian is an avid collector of antique marbles). What I saw in the corner of an antiques store there—a breathtaking display of vintage handkerchiefs—changed my life forever.

I remember that day as if it were yesterday. I heard the music of a hundred-piece orchestra in my head! Here were my vintage hankies, my vintage treasures! Flowers mated expertly with scallop borders! Romantic roses lit up by enchanting vines! Such a happy combination of elegance and élan! And so small!

When I saw these hankies lying on the shelves, I was smitten with these tiny wild bursts of color and pattern. So much detail in such little squares! I bought more than one hundred of them on the spot. My first thought was: These will make the most amazing doll dresses. I was lit up. I was on fire.

The most incredible thing was that there were no two alike! Where can you go anywhere these days and find only one of something? In all my years of collecting, I have seen the same design on a hankie

only a couple of times. (And in keeping with my high standards, I would never make two of the same dress, even if I had two identical hankies.)

After my trip, I could not wait to get home and devour my hankies. The second I walked in the door,

I washed all of them by hand. Then I lovingly ironed them, making sure the corners were straight and that there were no scallops sticking up. I picked one and stared at it and thought: What is the best way to cut this hankie and show it off to its full potential? What is the best way to keep the integrity of the hankie intact, yet make it extra special?

Thoughts kept coming at me from all directions. I had to consider the size of the hankie, the depth of the border, the amount of solid color in the center. Could I get a hat or purse out of the hankie? Could I make a bodice that was interesting and detailed? Would long or short sleeves work better with a scallop border? What is the best length to make the skirt so that I'm not chopping off the prettiest part of the print? What notion, if any, can be added for embellishment? Everything is so small on this scale: there is no room for error. One eighth of an inch is like a foot in the real world. A person needs a lot of expertise to make something in miniature because allowing even the tiniest fraction too much or too little at a seam throws off the whole dress.

My goal was to make a dress that would complement its "mother"—the handkerchief it was born from. I also wanted to create something that would be fun to play with. I have seen the way doll clothes are made today, and it is appalling—cheap polyester fabric, Velcro that is barely stitched on—how can

OPPOSITE PAGE AND NEAR LEFT: These are some of the cute vintage hankies that inspire my creativity—of course there are no ugly hankies!

anyone have fun playing with anything so poorly made?

I kept making hankie dresses by the dozen, all the while keeping out the choicest examples for my private collection—a.k.a. the Wall of Fame. I hoped someday to publish a book that would show off these specially selected dresses. Sometimes, in my zealousness to create, I would forget to take a picture of the uncut hankie before I made it into a dress! Oops! Too late! That's why some of the dresses in these pages are shown with the hankie they were made from, and some are just shown by themselves.

My love for my dresses grew as I continued to make them. Eventually, I had one hundred dresses. They were all magnificent and special! But I realized that this was not enough for a book. In time, I had two hundred dresses. I could not part with a single one. Then three hundred dresses! Four hundred dresses! Such gorgeous hankies, one prettier than the next! Five hundred dresses! What started out on little doll racks was now taking up an

LEFT: This bewitching autumn foliage gown was one of my first Hankie Couture creations.

By Marsha

ABOVE: This picture shows my first woven label. The other side says "Hankie Panky," which was my original designer doll dress label. I've since changed it to Hankie Couture, a more perfect name for my collection. But there are thousands of dresses out there with the "Hankie Panky by Marsha" label sewn in the dress.

RIGHT: My Wall of Fame showcases more than six hundred one-of-a-kind dresses from my private collection. It represents five years of searching, designing, cutting, and sewing.

entire wall. Six hundred dresses! No end in sight!

Then, more inspiration struck. I began looking at embroidered linens, tea towels, table runners, antimacassars, lace doilies, and small tablecloths as a source of ideas. These beautifully crafted pieces were stunning. After all, I knew what it took to make them—the French knots, the hand-crocheted edgings, the tiny cross-stitches. I had spent the last thirty years doing similar work. These beautiful pieces, when worked into the design of my hankie dresses, now form the basis of my ACEs chapter—appliqué, crochet, and embroidery (so aptly named by my wonderful husband, Brian).

Shortly thereafter, I sold my very first vintage hankie dress on eBay. I remember the moment exactly. It sold for twenty-eight dollars and was bought by a man named Robert. I jumped out of my chair and started hopping around the room! I knew my dreams and visions for these vintage treasures would become a reality someday.

But the *really* fun part of this

whole process is sitting down to sew the hankie dress. That's why I decided, after keeping my "trade secrets" to myself for such a long time, to finally break down and provide collectors and fans with simple patterns and instructions (see page 140) for making their own

LEFT: This "dashing" dress-and-coat ensemble (its original uncut hankie appears at right) demonstrates how a fun doll dress can be styled from a handkerchief.

hankie creations. After all, I want other people to share in the fun, too—even if having this much fun should be illegal! Seeing your ideas take shape, seeing your original vision become an actual dress that you can see and touch—there's no other feeling like it in the world!

When I sit down to sew, I become this obsessed crazy woman hunched over the sewing machine. (Don't even try to talk to me while I'm at the machine . . . If the phone rings, tough luck! You want dinner?! Go out!)

Whenever I buckle down to work, I always know before I cut the hankie what the end result will look like—I "see" it in my mind. Still, I take nothing for granted and I fit every single dress to the doll before I sew on the snaps (my least favorite job). I embellish my dresses by hand with buttons, Austrian crystals, rhinestones, vintage jewelry, gold chains, my own embroidery, feathers, tulle, flowers, roses, seashells, sequins, pearls, my very own floral hatbands, satin belts, contrast piping, pockets, hats, purses, umbrellas, and shoulder pads. Yes, tiny shoulder pads! I want to make each and every dress a complete fashion statement.

The best part of my dresses is that they are meant to be played with. As a result, they are durable and crafted with great attention to detail. I overlock

I normally remove vintage handkerchief labels like these when I find them still attached to the hankie. I call these hankies "pristine," as they have never been used or washed. Most hankies, however, do not have the label.

all my seams. I hand-stitch hems when necessary. I apply two sets of snaps on each dress (except on strapless dresses, which require only one snap). I back-stitch my seams for strength. All my dresses have pure cotton linings. The white linings make the hankie colors "pop" and they add strength to the dress. I put the same workmanship into my doll dresses that I would put into my real-life designer creations.

Many of the hankies I buy are in pristine condition. I'm amazed in my hunts that I can still find unused hankies with the original tags attached. But even hankies that are not a "perfect 10" can be

twinned with other hankies. Sometimes I search for a new cotton "sister" fabric for a vintage hankie that complements the look of the dress.

One day I realized that I needed a special doll for my special dresses. I wanted to have my very own doll made—one that would capture the essence of Hankie Couture. My hankie doll had to be glamorous yet look demure and lovely. I wanted her to look sexy yet modest, youthful and fresh, and with a terrific sense of humor. So I found a toy company in China who could custom-make the doll I wanted. One thousand emails later, I finally approved the prototype for production. The result is the doll who so winsomely models the fashions on the following pages.

It has always been important to me to

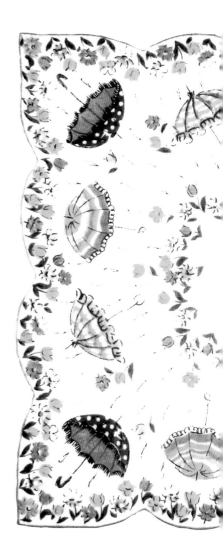

This playful lined raincoat, scarf, and matching parasol are pictured with their source—the original uncut hankie.

be original, and nothing fits the bill so much as these charming doll dresses. Each one is made from a vintage hankie, and each hankie is one of a kind. In addition, the style and cut of the dress is unique to that particular hankie, and that design will never be repeated—ever. Even after the creation of more than four thousand hankie dresses—including the design, the strategic planning, cutting, sewing, embellishing, and selling—I won't sit down at the cutting table unless I can figure out a way to cut each hankie in a brand new style.

Many people have written to me asking if I could fashion a dress out of their grandmother's hankie, or another relative's hankie that they've had sitting in a drawer. People have sent me their deceased sister's hankie, their aunt's

hankie, their cherished mother's hankie, and I'm proud that I've been able to give them back something that can be played with and enjoyed. I think it's because my dresses strike a chord in people's hearts. They evoke a fond memory. People feel and see the love that I have put into my dresses. The dresses speak for themselves.

I believe women enjoy dressing up—the more outfits, the more fun! And—if only in the imagination—what better way to have fun than with these vintage treasures? The dresses conjure up opportunities for play no

This roller-skating prima ballerina does it all—she skates, she pirouettes, and she wears a beaded tiara as she gives astrology advice on wheels. What a gal!

matter what your age. Each one suggests an occasion, an event, a fantasy. The designs, the romance, and all the matching components feed the imagination.

To all you creative and inventive people out there—especially designers, artists, and collectors—this book is for you! It's also for sewing hobbyists and all those who appreciate excellent craftsmanship. In addition, this book is for those whose vision gives my dresses life as they wear them in their minds and fasten them on their dolls. Lastly, this book is for the obsessed: only they can know the reasons behind my passion for transforming handkerchiefs into art in the first place.

Hankie Couture can be summed up in this one sentence: "When you look good, you feel good!" And when you feel good, there is a sweet, carefree, spontaneous, lighthearted fullness that fills your soul! So, dear reader, turn the pages and enjoy. Even when you just pretend to wear these dresses, you are making my dream come true.

ABOVE LEFT: I joined three hankies together for this pretty homage-to-Mother dress.

ABOVE RGHT: I was able to make this four-piece ensemble from a single hankie!

1

The Hankie Dress

THE ORIGINAL VINTAGE-HANKIE CREATION

Here is where it all began: the vintage hankie dress. Like a theme introducing its variations, the "pure" vintage hankie dress serves as an inspiration—the mother of invention, so to speak. Each individual dress in this chapter was made entirely from one vintage hankie. That is, the dresses have no added fabrics except the new all-cotton lining underneath. Even the accessories for any given dress are made from the same single vintage hankie. The details can include fancy collars, fitted waists, cap sleeves, sewn-in sleeves, belts, and hats. Each dress is without equal— an anomaly, in a very good way!

Never underestimate the
power
of a
Hankie Couture
woman.

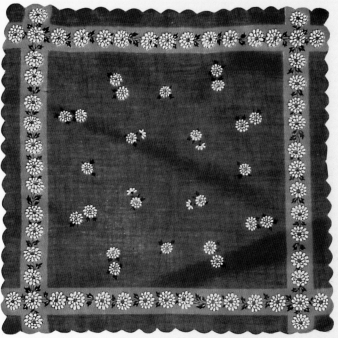

From the Hankie Couture
Motivational Manual:
Give yourself

artistic

license—but always
be punctual.

Hankie Couture girls
possess the gift of

style:

they are surprising,
not obvious, in their dress;
they are spontaneous,
but not impulsive.

The mere presence of a Hankie Couture woman serves as an inspiration. Others are drawn to her *buoyant* personality.

The elements of the

perfect

Hankie Couture wardrobe:
Pretty vintage dresses . . .
Matching millinery . . .
Purses . . . Pumps . . . Pearls!

Hankie Couture women have
an unquenchable thirst for the

fabulous.

They admit it—
they like their stuff!

The world of Hankie Couture
has room for everyone.
It's the town everyone likes to call

home.

Animals and people coexist peacefully
in the Hankie Couture world.
Each treasures the other's

loyal

companionship.

Hankie Couture
women are never extreme.
They always
follow the rules of good
taste
and femininity.

The elements of the perfect
Hankie Couture dress:
A headline-making hemline . . .
A well-defined waist . . .
A flattering neckline . . .
Plenty of
trimmings!

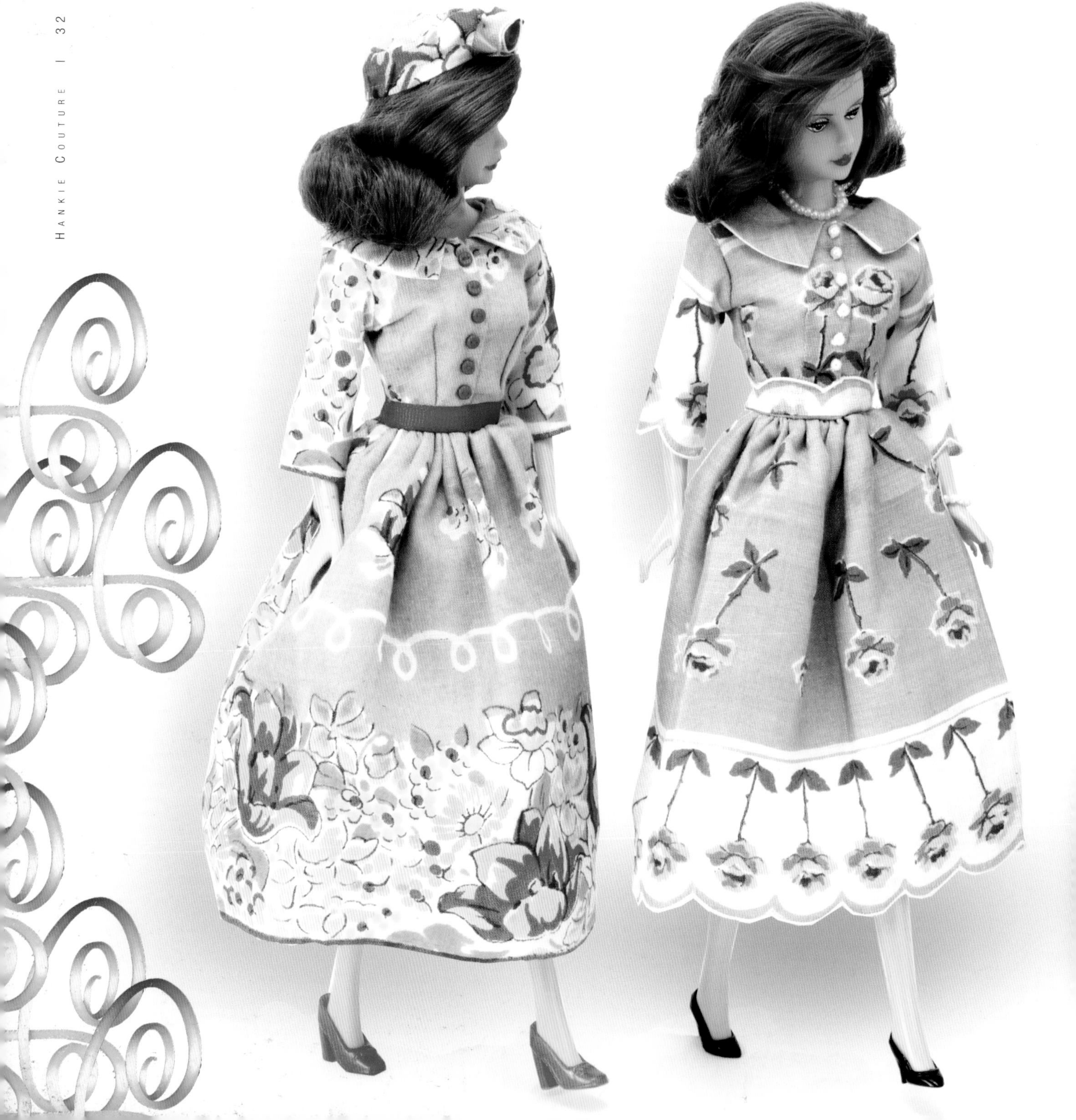

A Hankie Couture woman
knows that all friendships
require careful maintenance.
That's why she's
adored
by so many!

A Hankie Couture
woman is an

architect

of fashion: she designs
dresses from the building
blocks of color,
line, and symmetry.

A Hankie Couture woman's

authenticity

cannot be denied.
She reveals her honest self to
everyone she meets.

2

The Apron Dress

HANKIES
TWINNED WITH
COMPLEMENTARY
FABRICS

These dresses pair an original vintage hankie with either a different vintage hankie or a new complementary all-cotton print or solid fabric. The addition of the second hankie or subtle print allows me to showcase the beauty of the "main" hankie and to devise new ways to cut and position it—often as an "apron" over the underlying dress. This makes my strategic design all the more important! By adding this extra hankie or fabric I can give myself more creative freedom and invent even more new and intriguing styles.

What fuels a Hankie Couture woman's boundless energy? Courage, persistence, and plenty of *moxie!*

Serendipity

plays a
role in every
Hankie Couture
woman's daily life.

A beautiful Hankie
Couture dress is the seed
from which pure
intimacy
is sown.

The women of Hankie Couture realize
that life is filled with

pleasure.

There is real joy in being alive!

The ladies of Hankie Couture
greet each morning with a
spring
in their step. They believe in the
promise of the day to come.

Hankie Couture girls are
forward-looking.
Why hesitate? Their

attitude

lets others know
that Hankie Couture girls
can't go wrong.

In the Hankie Couture
world, good
manners
are easy to come by.
Politeness is the universal
currency.

Entries under S in the
Hankie Couture dictionary:

Spontaneous . . .

Simple . . .

Serene . . .

Sophisticated . . .

Savvy!

The women of Hankie Couture take their cue from *nature* and its infinite patterns, reflecting their respect for all living things.

What gives a Hankie Couture woman that "wow" factor? Her *passion* for life!

Hankie Couture women spend plenty of time

daydreaming.

There's no
such thing as a waste
of time, because
time is in abundant supply.

The Hankie Couture
commandments:
Be flexible . . .
Be articulate . . .
Be forgiving . . .
Be
cheerful!

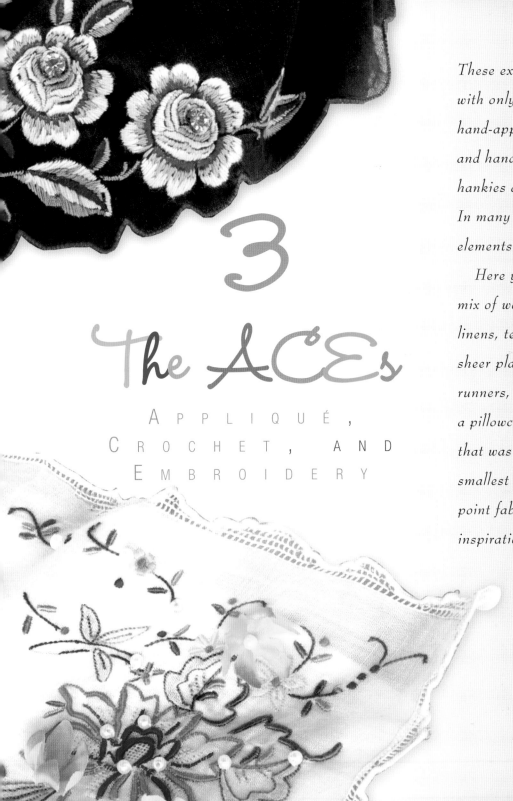

3
The ACEs

APPLIQUÉ,
CROCHET, AND
EMBROIDERY

These exceptional dresses are sewn with only the most phenomenal hand-appliquéd, hand-crocheted, and hand-embroidered vintage hankies and linens I could find. In many creations, I mixed all three elements for spectacular results.

Here you'll find a truly eclectic mix of wonderful vintage hankies, linens, tea towels, an antique sheer place mat, small table runners, wine coasters, and even a pillowcase! There is one dress that was made from just the smallest morsel of antique petit point fabric. Who knows where inspiration will come from?

Hankie Couture
women understand the
importance of being

unique.

They appreciate the
value of a one-of-
a-kind, inimitable
artistic achievement.

Hankie Couture has a reputation for
sweetness and respectability.
The women who wear it attract many

loyal

friends and admirers.

Hankie Couture girls are attracted
to voluminous, unapologetically
overflowing skirts.
They drape beautifully
and make a

sensuous

playground for
the eye.

It's easy for a
Hankie Couture woman
to look like a

goddess,

because she
knows her beauty is
appreciated.

The Hankie Couture woman is always

meticulously

groomed. She derives

immense satisfaction from her

daily beauty regimen.

Hankie Couture ladies believe that there's a place for everything, and everything has its place. Life is much

easier

when you're organized.

A Hankie Couture woman's top priorities:

Create *drama...*

Listen well . . .

Do it right . . .

Embrace the moment!

Every Hankie Couture
woman knows that
the smallest

details

make the biggest
difference.

A Hankie Couture
woman is
blessed
with an intuitive
mind. She stays fully
in tune with
the laws of nature.

A Hankie Couture woman possesses a **keen** intellect. She makes an effort to learn something new every day.

A Hankie Couture woman feels

at home

in any setting.

Her attitude is truly

cosmopolitan.

Every Hankie Couture
woman is a skilled
couturier. She can whip up
a dress in the morning and

amaze

an audience with it that
very night.

The women of Hankie Couture
easily succumb to the charms
of a profusion of

color.

They draw energy from nature's
brilliant kaleidoscope.

Hankie Couture
women
embrace
the lost art
of casual
correspondence.
Each day,
they write a letter
or phone
a friend
just to
say hello.

HEARTY BIRTHDAY GREETINGS

BIRTHDAY GREETING.
Here's Good Luck and best of health,
With a goodly store of wealth
And Love, like summer flowers,
future hours.

It's always spring in the world of Hankie Couture. The **blooming** season lasts year-round.

4
Sleek and Sophisticated

ELEGANT
ENSEMBLES
WITH
COSMOPOLITAN
FLAIR

These haute hankie styles feature dresses that fit close to the body, or have a special detail that makes them perfect for businesswomen or urbane trendsetters.

Many of these chic ensembles presented a bit more of a challenge in the sewing process than an ordinary vintage hankie dress, especially the three-piece fitted suits—what with all the hand-cut piping, compact fit, tiny ruffles, and tiny cuffs. Some of them took as much time to make as an adult tailored suit. But they were worth it, because every Hankie Couture woman needs a little "uptown" in her wardrobe!

Hankie Couture girls insist on a *proper* fit—close, but not tight—especially when it comes to slim-fitting skirts that circle sleekly around the hips.

Hankie Couture girls enjoy a cosmopolitan view of fashion. Their fondness for fine fabrics makes them designers of a special kind—creators of their own universe of *chic.*

A Hankie Couture
woman never runs out
of ideas. She leads
fearlessly, always in
charge and

sure

of her direction.

There are four ways to carry a hankie:

Neatly

folded in your purse . . .

Peeking out from inside a glove . . .

Loosely tied around your wrist . . .

Carefully tucked in your décolletage!

The contents of a
Hankie Couture woman's purse:
A flacon of

perfume...

A tube of lipstick . . .
A tortoiseshell comb . . .
A carefully folded hankie . . .
A drawstring bag of peppermints!

The women of Hankie Couture bring *beauty* to life.

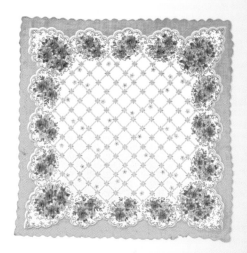

Friends who share common
goals—like the enjoyment
of Hankie Couture—
stay together
forever.

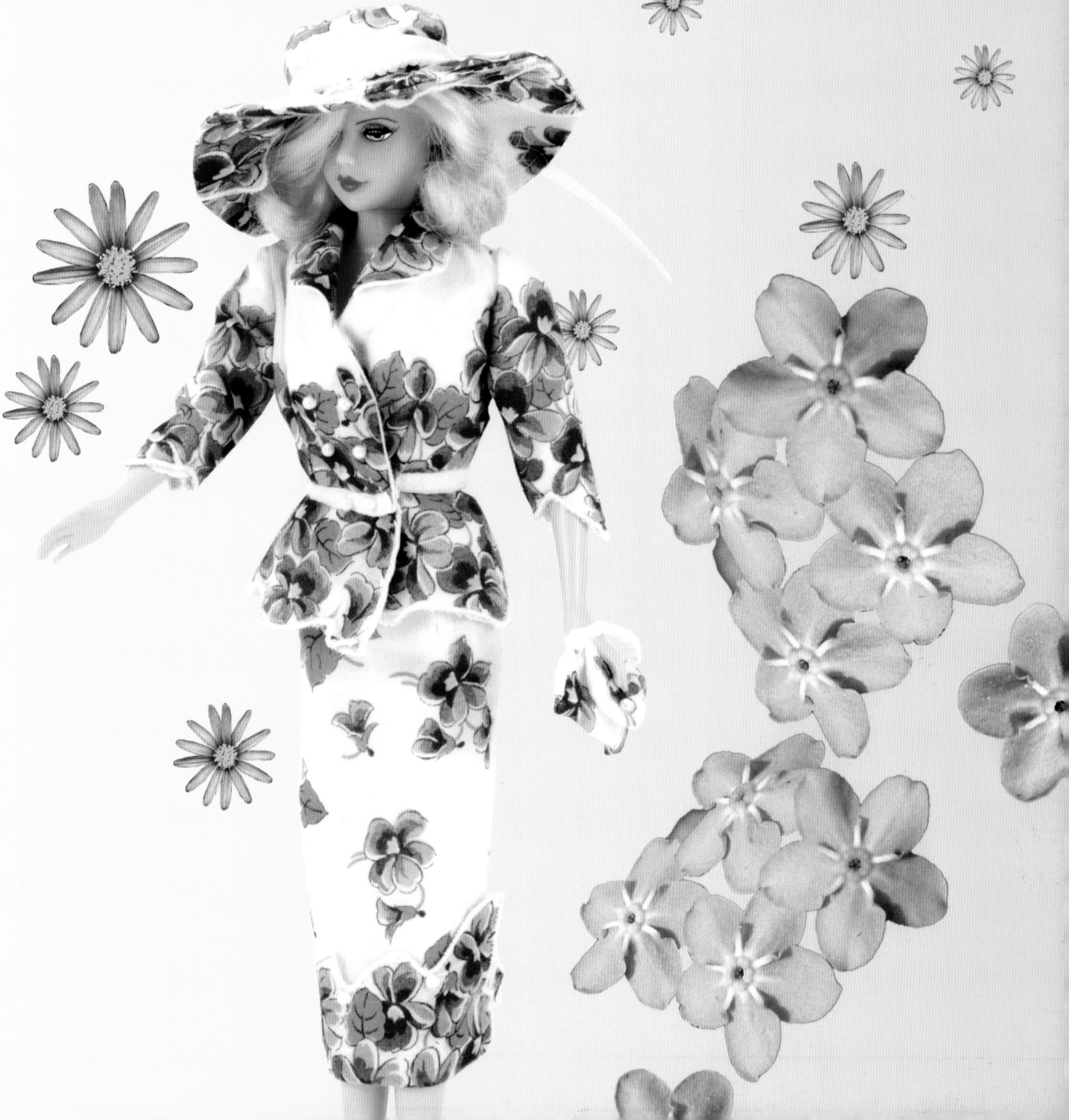

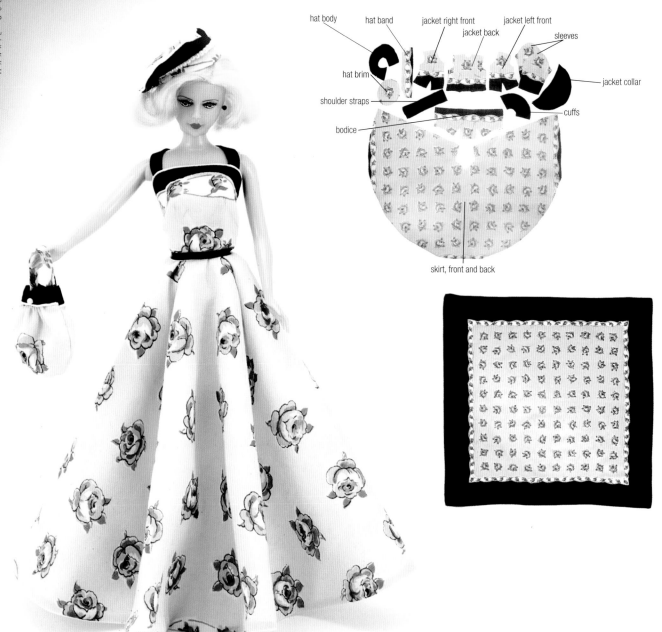

hat body

hat band

jacket right front

jacket left front

jacket back

sleeves

hat brim

jacket collar

shoulder straps

cuffs

bodice

skirt, front and back

Custom-made couture

is a Hankie Couture woman's bread and butter.
Nothing else provides the perfect combination
of fit, style, and flattering lines.

The women of Hankie Couture
know that good taste is

timeless.

A Hankie Couture woman

commands

attention.

All eyes are riveted on her.

A Hankie Couture woman starts
the morning with a

brainstorm—

then harvests the results all day.

5

Just for Fun!

DRESSES WITH A SENSE OF HUMOR

These dresses are made from vintage hankies that depict humorous, lighthearted messages or scenes, including people and animals. This was an especially fun chapter for me, as these hankies appealed to my playful side! They had such gaiety and tomfoolery about them; they were practically begging me to use them to create something equally whimsical and witty. I actually did laugh out loud when I was cutting some of these precious little hankies, and can only imagine the joy the hankies gave to their original owners. Wouldn't it be wonderful if such treasures were still manufactured today?

Custom-made Hankie Couture is a smart woman's personal

signature.

Nothing else provides the same fit, wit, and touch of

fantasy.

The women of Hankie Couture are keenly aware that looking good and feeling good go hand in hand. The

confidence

born from an attractive appearance travels from the outside all the way in, straight to the heart.

CALORIES
VITAMINS
CALORIES
300 CALORIES
CHEST
THIGHS
HIPS
LEGS
NECK
ARMS
KEEP SLIM

Hankie Couture ladies have taken
the word "normal" out of their vocabularies
and replaced it with the words

"imaginative,"

"artistic," and "inspired."
These ladies speak the language of
originality and creativity.

Hankie Couture women radiate a
captivating
inner light.
They give of themselves so that
others may dream.

The ladies of Hankie Couture
love to travel.

Blue skies

follow them wherever they go.

You can tell a Hankie Couture woman by her hat. It's the one with the distinctive

embellishments.

Hankie Couture women
prefer dresses with a touch of

whimsy.

In eccentricity lies the seed of
the truly divine!

Hankie Couture women fill
their leisure time with

intelligent

pursuits, such as the care
and conservation
of natural resources.

Entries under F in the Hankie
Couture Dictionary:

Fabulous...

Fantastic . . .

Fervent . . .

Finesse . . .

Flair!

A Hankie Couture woman
brings the gift of
effortless
humor to any social gathering.

Hankie Couture
stimulates the senses.
The rustle of a
skirt, the scent of a
gardenia, a

knowing

glance, the
caress of a flower
petal, the sweet
tang of a sun-warmed
strawberry . . .

6

Special Occasions

WEDDINGS, PARTIES, AND CELEBRATIONS

Here's where you'll find the perfect ensemble for weddings, engagements, birthday or anniversary parties, public appearances, or any other high-profile event. I've chosen to showcase mostly floor-length gowns, but I've also included some tea-length dresses—all extravagant in design, suitable for making a grandiose entrance. Many of them have Austrian crystals hand-sewn to the fabric, with the added embellishment of bits of lace and pearls. Each and every one of them is ready for a close-up!

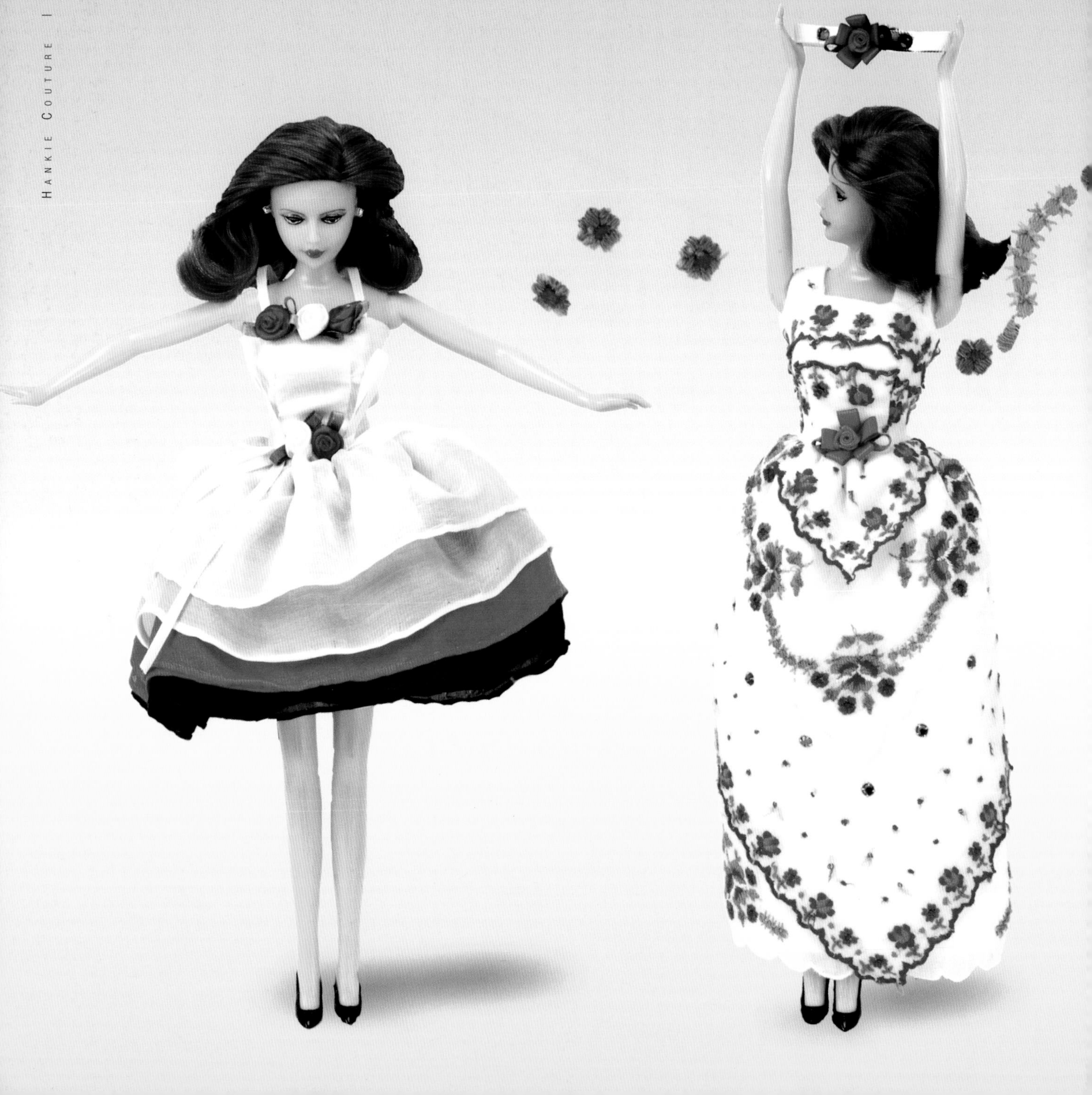

Ah, the virtues of a Hankie
Couture girl! She possesses an

indomitable

spark, and her style crackles
with wit!

Hankie Couture
imparts an air of
refinement
and privilege.

How to wear Hankie Couture:
Aim for understatement, but
keep the accents bold . . .
Combine simplicity of cut with

opulence

of detail for an outstanding
silhouette!

Once upon a time,
there were five girlfriends
who grew up together. They shared their
precious childhood, their adventurous
teen years, and, finally, their young
adulthood. Their names were Shari,
Marsha, Rose, Ida, and Isabel.

At long last, the day arrived
when Shari was to become a bride!
Her friends, with whom she had
shared cuts and bruises, homework,
shopping excursions, and countless
meals, were thrilled for her.

Marsha

was to be the maid of
honor. On the day of
the wedding, she made
sure that Shari looked
perfect. She smoothed her
dress and paid particular
attention to the drape of
the fabric. She wanted it
to look nice and full.

Rose

was to be a bridesmaid. She was so loyal! On the wedding day, she concerned herself with Shari's headpiece. Her main interest was the tender care of the flowers, as they were just picked and so fresh!

Finally, the moment approached for the tossing of the bouquet. *Shari* took one long look at her lovely friends, turned around, closed her eyes, and threw the flowers over her shoulder. Who was the lucky bridesmaid?

To this day, the friends won't tell. They gathered in a circle and held on to the bouquet, each one touching part of it. It was if they all participated in its promise of joy. Shari enjoyed a long, happy marriage, and she and her friends lived lives of peace and fulfillment every day thereafter. It was truly a beautiful wedding.

A Hankie Couture
woman gives her best
performance
each time the curtain rises.
After all, the

star

hangs above her
dressing-room door!

Hankie Couture girls are a

spirited

bunch, ready for anything. Their
straightforward approach gets them
where they want to go—fast!

The
cultured
ladies of Hankie Couture
approach the art of getting
dressed with an intimate
knowledge of curvature,
folds, and form. They know
how to use turns and twists of
fabric to create a symphony
of light and shadow.

Dazzle alert: The *glitter* of Hankie Couture is coming this way.

7

Sleepwear

PLAYFUL
AND
LOVELY

This chapter features a variety of looks for bedtime, from peek-a-boo PJs to glamorous peignoirs. Of all my creations— and I love every single one of them—these are the ones whose designs I can envision fitting most easily into present-day lifestyles. Contemporary women would wear these feminine confections in a heartbeat— while lounging around the house, having tea, preparing for bed, and even sleeping. These sexy, daring, and provocative little numbers were a blast to create— and I bet they would be even more fun to wear!

The women of
Hankie Couture
know that

charm

is a virtue.

Hankie Couture girls
relish time spent in their
dressing rooms and
boudoirs. It gives them a
feeling of
balance,
grace, and harmony,
so they can go forth and
greet the world
with poise and good cheer.

Six ways to unwind after
a long, active day:
Breathe
deeply . . .
Compose yourself . . .
Collect yourself . . .
Stretch . . .
Smell the flowers . . .
Congratulate yourself on
a job well done!

The women of
Hankie Couture
maintain
a healthy
perspective on life.
They recognize

laughter

as therapy.

Every Hankie Couture woman
knows the importance of the

five R's:

Rejuvenate . . .

Rejoice . . .

Release . . .

Refresh . . .

Relax!

Hankie Couture nights call for
a special kind of glamour—
subtle, innocent,

nonchalant.

A Hankie Couture woman
goes to bed each night with a

smile

in her heart.

Hankie Couture
women walk

confidently.

Their stride creates a
pleasing rhythm with every
surefooted step.

Hankie Couture women
approach first impressions
with care. Their secret?
The playful

twinkle

in their eyes.

In the world of Hankie
Couture, there's nothing
wrong with a little coy
flirtation
now and then.

Hankie Couture women
add a spoonful of
novelty
and
excitement to
everything
they do.

Hankie Couture
women appreciate
down time.
That's when they

enjoy

their PPMs—pure
pleasure moments!

Breakfast is one of a
Hankie Couture woman's
greatest pleasures.
The food that nourishes the
body also nourishes the
soul.

Restful sleep requires
the right kind of
Hankie Couture
nightgown. Bows, lace,
and embroidery set the
mood for

tranquil

slumber.

In the world of Hankie Couture, everything matters. There's no such thing as a small achievement when you've put your *heart* and soul into the effort.

This chapter is for those of you who feel inspired to sew your own vintage-hankie doll dress. If you have a special hankie from your mom or grandmother, this might be the perfect time to take it out of the drawer and make something with it. In fact, some of my favorite dresses in this book were made from hankies that were given to me or passed on to me from my mom. But if you don't want to use a family heirloom to make your own hankie creation, then browse for hankies at your local antiques store, flea market, or at garage sales—that's where I found many of the vintage hankies I used in this book. You never know where you'll spot something that gets your creative juices flowing!

These directions tell you how to make my most basic hankie dress—a lined strapless style with a full skirt, fitted bodice, bust darts, and an optional ribbon at the waist. It's a good style for beginning sewers. More advanced sewers should feel free to use a hankie with a scalloped border, or look through this book for additional styling ideas.

I recommend reading the directions several times before you begin so that you can thoroughly familiarize yourself with the process. **Remember—measure twice and cut once!** Depending on your sewing skills, the dress can take anywhere from one to two hours to make. Have fun, and happy sewing!

8
How-To

INSTRUCTIONS FOR MAKING YOUR VERY OWN HANKIE DOLL DRESS

MATERIALS YOU WILL NEED

One handkerchief, approximately 12 inches square

³⁄₈ yard white 100% cotton fabric for lining

Small sewing needle

All-purpose mercerized cotton thread to coordinate with color of hankie

All-purpose mercerized cotton thread in a contrasting color for basting and for the tailor tack

Ruler

Scissors

One 8½ x 11-inch sheet tracing paper

Pencil with a dark, soft lead

Straight pins

Steam or dry iron and ironing board

Small snap for back closure

Sewing machine (optional)

BUT WHERE DO YOU FIND VINTAGE HANKIES?

- *Antique malls and antique stores*
- *Antique swap meets across the country*
- *Flea markets across the country*
- *Estate and garage sales*
- *eBay auctions*
- *Aunt Isabel's dresser drawer!*
- *Grandma's attic*

Keep in Mind . . .

- All **seams** should be **¼ inch wide**.

- **Always cut** loose threads with scissors—
  do not pull them out by hand.

- **Pressing your garment** is as important
  as sewing it. This is the secret to making
  your hankie dress look exceptional!

- Whenever you pin two pieces together,
  make sure to place a pin at each corner
  and in the center, otherwise the pieces
  can slip out of alignment.

- It's very important to use **100% cotton** for
  the dress lining—other fabrics, such as nylon,
  will fray and will not have the proper opacity.

- Although this hankie dress can be sewn
  on a machine, some people will prefer to sew
  it by hand because of the **small scale of
  the garment.**

- See pages **47, 54, 93, 96, 104, 111, 112,
  117, and 118** for samples of this dress design
  and its variations.

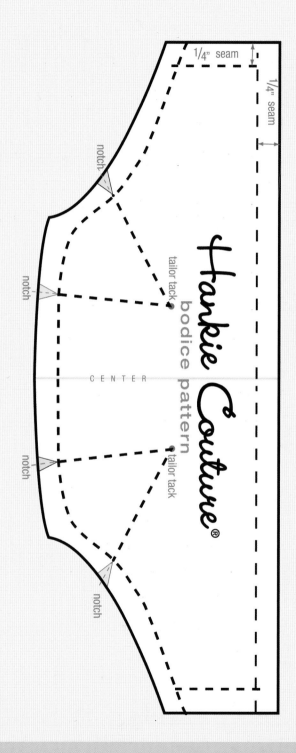

CUTTING OUT YOUR HANKIE DRESS

1 Lay the hankie over the cotton lining, making sure the bottom edges are even. Be sure to lay the hankie over the **selvage**, or smooth edge of the lining. Using your ruler, measure 5½ inches up from the bottom edge of the hankie. Mark the point with straight pins, as shown in the illustration, then cut across the entire hankie and lining together.

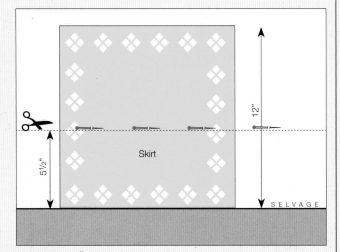

2 Next, cut the excess lining on both sides of the hankie, being careful not to cut the hankie itself. There! You have now cut out the skirt!

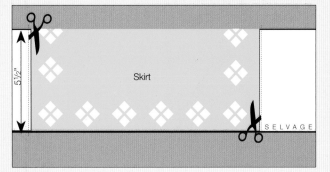

3 Now for the bodice: lay the tracing paper over **the bodice pattern on page 143.** Using your pencil, trace the pattern as neatly as possible onto the tracing paper and set aside. Be sure to trace the **notches**, seam lines, and points for **tailor tacks** as well.

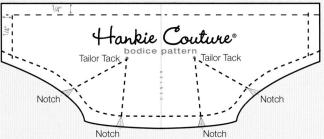

4 Then lay the remainder of the uncut hankie (not the part you're using for the skirt) over the remainder of the cotton lining. Next, lay the tracing paper with the pattern on it over the part of the hankie that you find the most colorful and pretty. Try to make the front of the bodice centered over the design. Pin the tracing paper to the hankie and cut the hankie and lining together around the edges of the paper.

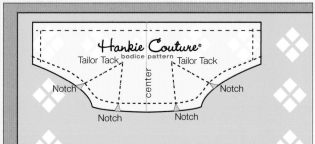

5 Very carefully, while the tracing paper is still pinned to the hankie and lining, cut **notches** at the bottom of the bodice where the pattern says **"notch"** (see Helpful Hints, page 158). Using a **tailor tack** (see Helpful Hints, page 158), mark the tip of the bust dart. Congratulations! You have now completed cutting out the hankie dress and are ready to create your masterpiece.

SEWING YOUR HANKIE DRESS

1 Hold the two bodice pieces (one cut from the hankie and the other cut from the lining material) with the right sides (not the wrong sides) together. Pin the lining to the bodice, then sew a seam across the straight edge of the bodice pieces.

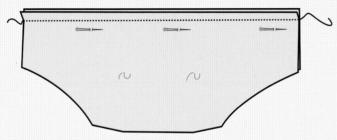

2 Fold the lining over so that it lies on top of the hankie's wrong side and, using your iron, press the edges together. **Baste** *(see Helpful Hints, page 158)* along the remaining edges of the bodice piece. Clip all loose threads.

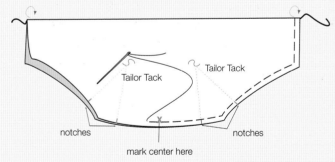

Tailor Tack

Tailor Tack

notches

notches

mark center here

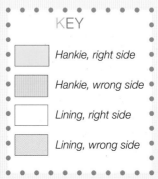

KEY

Hankie, right side

Hankie, wrong side

Lining, right side

Lining, wrong side

3 To make the darts, pin the seam lines together, with the right side of the lining facing you. Sew through both layers, stitching each dart from the wide end, where the notch is, to the dart point, where the tailor tack is. Don't forget to backstitch at the beginning and at the end of each dart! Using your iron, press the darts toward the center, then gently pull out the tailor tacks.

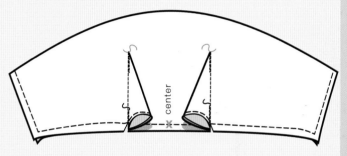

center

4 Now we return to the skirt. Sewing through both the hankie fabric and lining, sew two rows of gathering stitches at the top of the skirt, as shown in the illustration *(see Helpful Hints, page 158)*. Leave the ends of the thread on both rows of stitches unknotted.

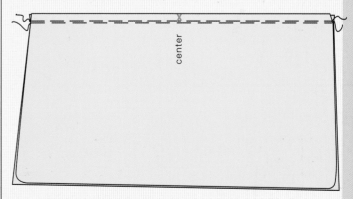

center

5 With the right sides together, pin the skirt to the bodice, matching centers.

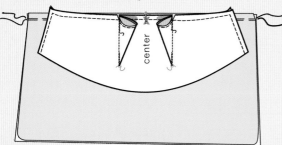

6 Pull the loose ends of thread on the gathering stitches and adjust to fit. Make sure both edges of the bodice are even with both edges of the skirt, then place pins to hold both sections together.

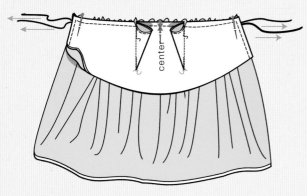

7 **Baste** the bodice and the skirt together, then sew. Using your iron, press the seam toward the bodice. We are almost done!

match center marks

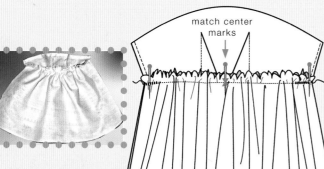

8 With the right sides together, create the center back seam of the skirt by stitching 4½ inches up from the bottom of the skirt. Don't forget to **reinforce your stitches** *(see Helpful Hints, page 156)* so the seam will not open up!

KEY

	Hankie, right side
	Hankie, wrong side
	Lining, right side
	Lining, wrong side

9 Now turn the hankie dress right side out. Isn't it pretty? Fit the dress on your doll, if you have one. Check to see where you want the snap to be placed at the back of the dress. Mark the desired location with a pin and sew the snap on. Cut and remove any basting stitches you see on the right side of the dress.

Optional: Sew a small ribbon and/or rosette to the center front at the waistline. Be sure to use a coordinating thread and don't let any stitches show through to the right side.

You did a great job creating something truly unique and beautiful. Enjoy your hankie treasure!

SEWING A ROUND NECK BODICE DRESS

Samples of this dress appear on pages 30, 48, 65, 86, 102, and 119.

Note: To cut the skirt, please refer to pattern pieces on page 155, steps 1 and 2. If you are using a hankie smaller than 12 x 12 inches, you will need to shorten the length of the skirt pattern to 4½ inches.

1 Stitch the darts on the bodice front. Using an iron, press toward center.

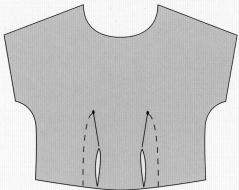

2 With right sides together, stitch the bodice front to the bodice back at the shoulders. Press the seam open. Prepare the lining in the same manner following steps 1 and 2.

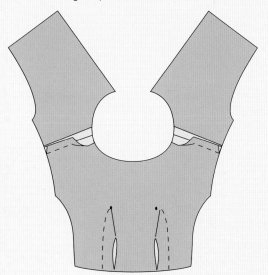

3 With right sides together, pin the lining to the bodice. Stitch the back and neck opening. Stitch the armhole edges.

The curves around the neck and armhole edges need to be clipped so that the bodice can be turned inside out. Clip at ¼-inch intervals, being very careful not to cut past the stitching line.

Turn the bodice inside out and press. Hint: to get a perfect pointed edge on the center back seams and neck edge, fold the center back bodice on the stitching lines, pinch the folded section tightly, then turn to the outside.

You may want to baste the raw edges together to hold the pieces together.

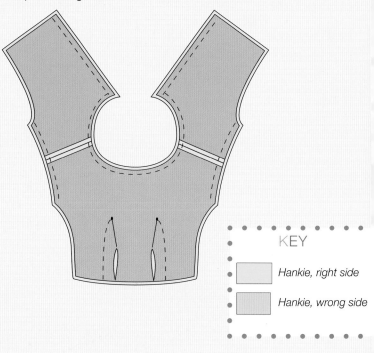

KEY	
	Hankie, right side
	Hankie, wrong side

4 With right sides together, stitch the bodice front and back together at the sides.

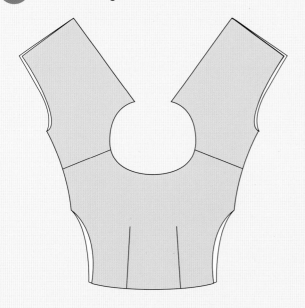

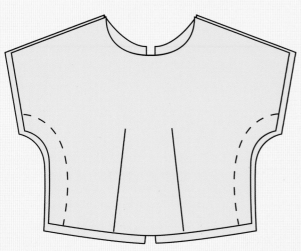

5 Gather the upper edge of the skirt with two rows of gathering stitches. Turn in seam allowance on both sides of the skirt.

6 With the right sides together, pin the skirt to the bodice matching centers. Adjust the gathers evenly, and then baste.
Sew. Press the seam gently toward the bodice.

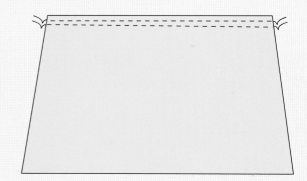

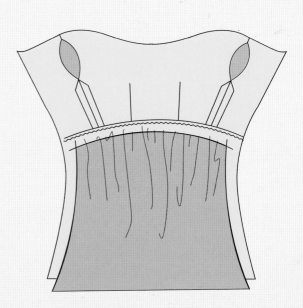

7 With the right sides together, create the center back seam of the skirt by stitching approximately 4½ inches up from the bottom of the skirt.

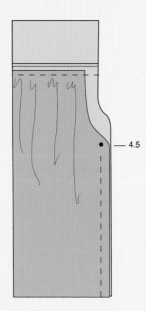

— 4.5

8 Sew the snaps to the back opening edges at the waist and upper back. Hint: For a perfect fit, it is a good idea to try the dress on the doll before you sew the snaps on.

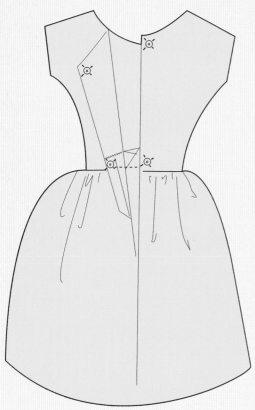

SEWING A SQUARE NECK BODICE DRESS

Samples of this dress appear on pages 44, 50, 57, 64, 66, 104, and 121.

Note: To cut the skirt, please refer to pattern piece on page 156.

1 Stitch the darts on the bodice front. Using an iron, press toward center.
Stitch the darts on the bodice lining. Using your iron, press toward center.

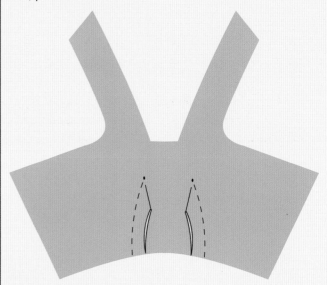

2 With right sides together, pin the lining to the bodice. Stitch the back, armhole, and neck edges, pivoting at the small black dots at the neckline. Make a small diagonal clip to small black dot. Be careful not to clip the stitches!
Clip around the curved armhole edges at ¼-inch intervals. Turn the bodice to right side, then press. I find it helpful to use a very strong pin, such as a quilter's pin, to turn the shoulder straps inside out. Be careful not to poke holes in the fabric. Proceed slowly!

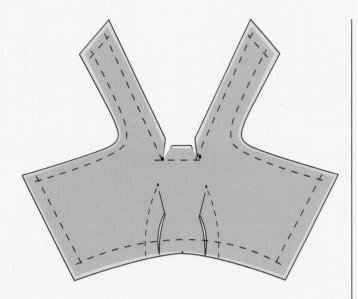

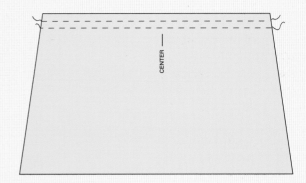

5 With the right sides together, pin the skirt to the bodice matching centers. Adjust the gathers evenly, and then baste. Sew. Press the seam toward the bodice.

3 Bring the straps to the inside back overlapping ¼ inch. Strap is sewn ⅞ inch from finished center back seam. Stitch straps in place.

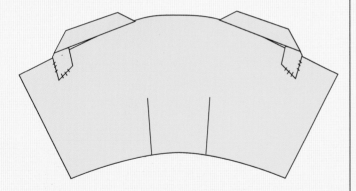

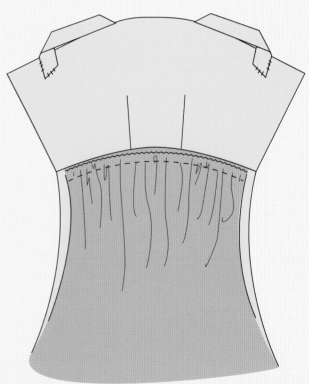

4 Gather the upper edge of the skirt with two rows of gathering stitches. Turn in seam allowance on both sides of the skirt. Press.

6 With right sides together, create the center back seam of the skirt by stitching approximately 4½ inches up from the bottom of the skirt.

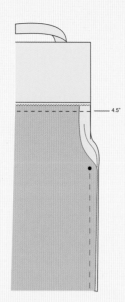

4.5"

7 Sew snaps to the back opening edges at the waist and upper back. It is a good idea to try the dress on the doll before you sew the snaps for a perfect fit!

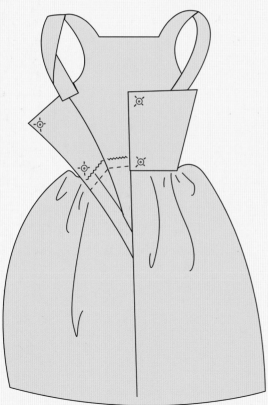

SEWING A CIRCULAR HAT

To cut the hat, please refer to pattern piece on page 157.

1 With right sides together, stitch around entire edge of the hat.

2 Clip the curves at ¼-inch intervals all the way around, being careful not to cut beyond the stitching lines.

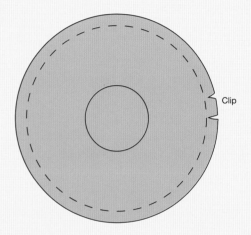

Clip

3 Turn the hat inside out and press flat.

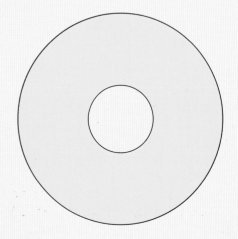

4 Stitch close to the inner edge of the circle.

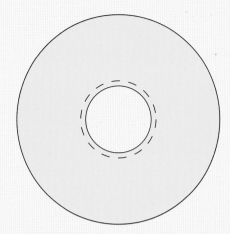

5 Using a zigzag stitch, zigzag around the inner edge.

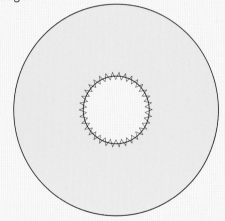

5 Try the hat on a doll. Adjust for fit. If the hat fits snuggly, make the inner circle edge a little bigger, by cutting ⅛ inch of the seam allowance. Zigzag over the cut edge.

At this point: flowers, beads, or pearls can be added to half of the inner circle edge. This will form a "crown" that is very flattering around your doll's head! Be sure to use enough flowers, beads, or pearls to cover at least half of the hat.

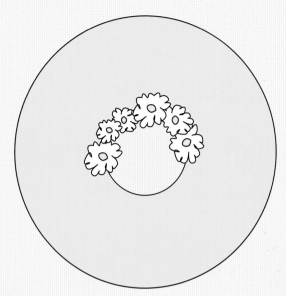

Variation

If you would like to add lace or piping to the outer edge of the hat, it must be added before you sew the hat sections together.

You will need approximately 14 inches of ½ inch wide trim. Pre-gathered lace trim or piping is a nice touch.

1 Make tiny cuts on the straight edge of your trim, less than ¼-inch deep.

2 Lay the trim on the right side of the hat using pins to keep the trim/lace in place. Baste around the entire edge.

3 Follow Steps 1–4 above to complete your hat.

SEWING A PURSE

To cut the purse, please refer to pattern piece on page 157.

1 With right sides together, stitch around entire edge, pivoting at corners. Leave a small opening along the bottom edge of the purse.

Make two small clips at the center fold line, being careful not to clip beyond the seam allowance.

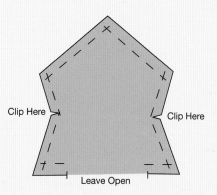

Clip Here

Clip Here

Leave Open

2 Turn the purse inside out. Hint: to get perfect pointed edges on this tiny purse, fold in the corners on the stitching lines, pinch the folded sections tightly together, and then turn to the outside. Use a strong needle to gently pull the corner out all the way. This will form a pointed edge. Using an iron, press flat.

Turn in the seam allowance on the bottom edge and stitch the opening closed.

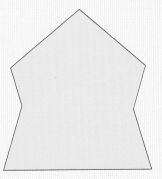

3 Fold the purse along the lower fold line and press. Stitch the sides of the purse close to the edge. If desired, you may stitch the sides of the purse by hand, using blind stitch.

Fold along the upper fold line to create the purse flap. Using an iron, press flat.

You may wish to embellish the purse flap by adding a pearl, bead, or rhinestone. If desired, you can also add a very small snap to the inside of the purse.

To create a shoulder strap, cut a ⅛ inch piece of ribbon 5 ½ inches long. Sew the ribbon to the inside edge of the purse, overlapping at least ¼ inch to the inside.

To create a clutch style purse that your doll can actually hold, cut a ¼-inch piece of elastic ¾ inch long. Sew the elastic to the back of the purse at each end, being careful to sew only through the back of the purse.

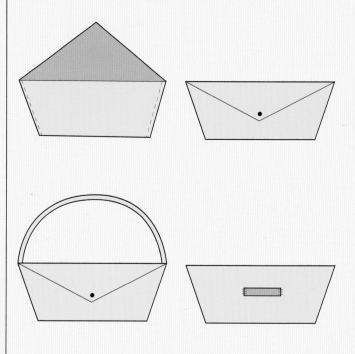

Additional pattern pieces

ROUND NECK
BODICE DRESS

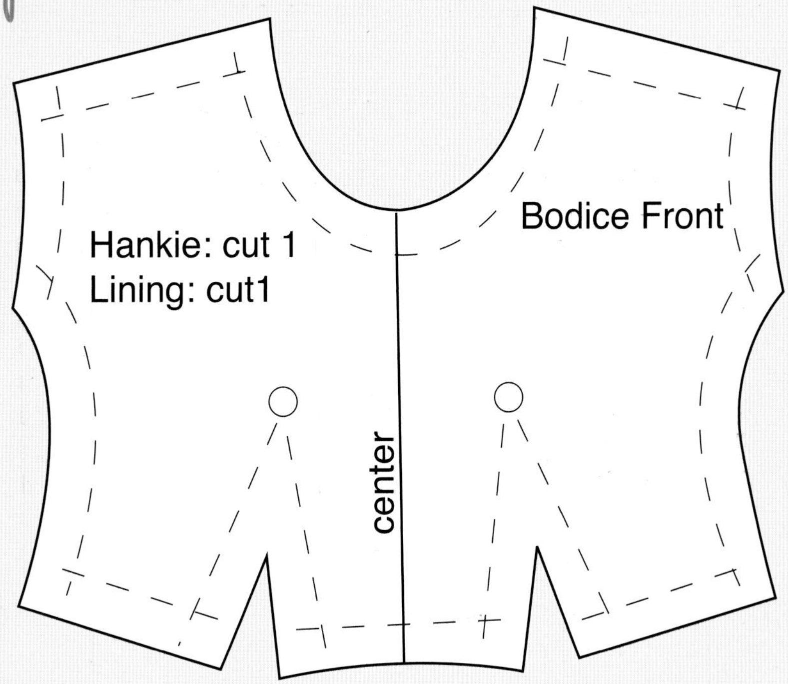

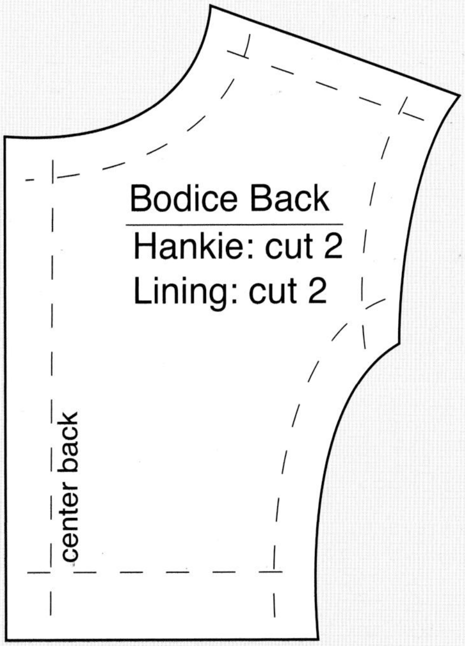

Hankie: cut 1
Lining: cut1

Bodice Front

center

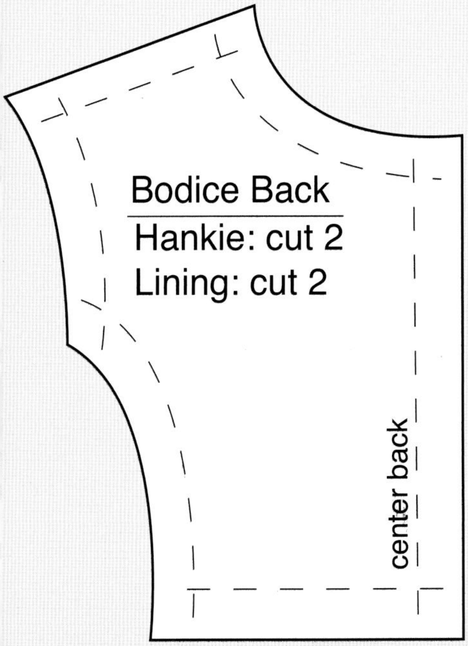

Bodice Back
Hankie: cut 2
Lining: cut 2

center back

Bodice Back
Hankie: cut 2
Lining: cut 2

center back

SQUARE NECK BODICE DRESS

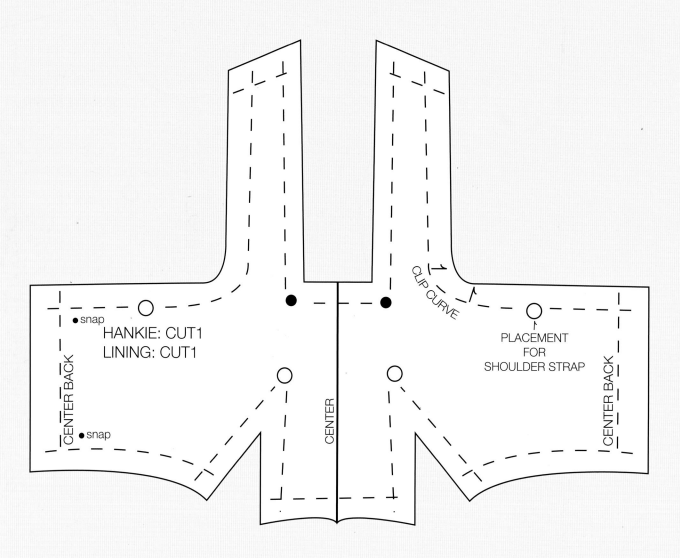

HANKIE: CUT1
LINING: CUT1

• snap

• snap

CENTER BACK

CENTER

CLIP CURVE

PLACEMENT
FOR
SHOULDER STRAP

CENTER BACK

PURSE

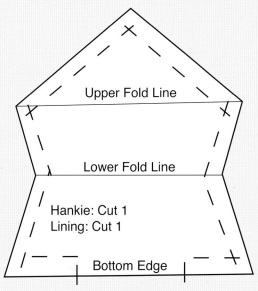

Upper Fold Line

Lower Fold Line

Hankie: Cut 1
Lining: Cut 1

Bottom Edge

CIRCULAR HAT

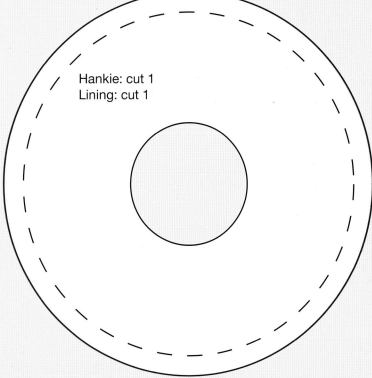

Hankie: cut 1
Lining: cut 1

Helpful Hints . . .

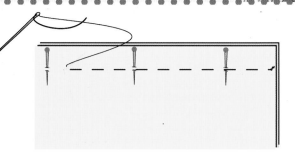

How to Baste

A basting stitch is a stitch made to loosely and temporarily attach two pieces of fabric together. Thread your needle with the contrasting-color thread (so you can easily see it and remember to remove it later). Make a knot at the end of the thread and weave the needle through the fabric, making long stitches of even lengths on both sides.

How to Gather

Gathering is used to create fullness. It may be done by hand or machine. If you do it by hand, use small stitches. If you do it by machine, set the machine to the longest stitch length. Whether you make the stitches by hand or by machine, it is easier to distribute the fullness evenly if there are at least two rows of gathering. Make your first row of stitches ¼ inch away from the raw edge—i.e., on the imaginary seam line. Cut the thread and leave it unknotted, then make your second row of stitches ⅛ inch above the first row—i.e., ⅛ inch away from the raw edge, inside the seam allowance. Cut the thread on the second row and leave it unknotted, too. To gather, pull the loose ends on both rows of thread with one hand as you push the fabric into folds of the desired size with the other hand.

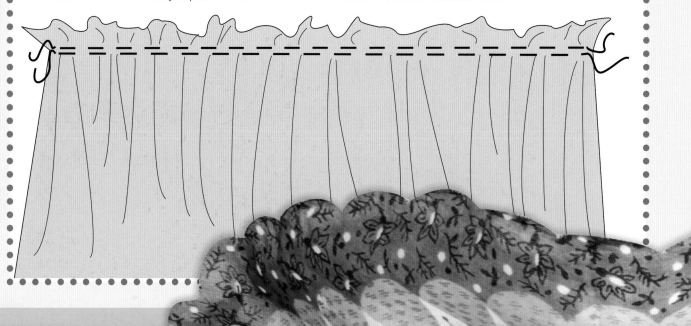

How to Cut a Notch

With the tracing-paper bodice pattern pinned to the fabric, use your scissors to make a 1/8-inch-long cut through the pattern and the fabric where the pattern is marked "notch." **Do not cut beyond the seam allowance.**

This will ensure that your cuts do not show in the finished dress.

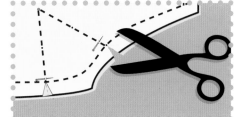

How to Reinforce a Seam

All seams and darts should be secured with extra stitches at the beginning and at the end. This prevents the thread from pulling out and strengthens the dress overall. As you begin sewing, **after 5 or 6 stitches, run the machine backward for 5 or 6 stitches, then move forward again**. Repeat the procedure when you reach 5 or 6 stitches from the end. If you're sewing by hand, then sew several stitches in place at the beginning and at the end. Make a double knot in the thread at the end of the seam or dart.

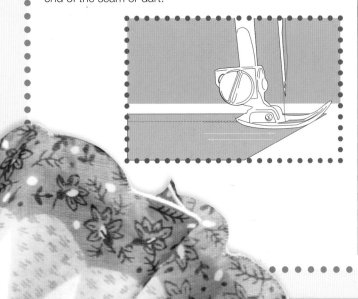

How to Make a Tailor Tack

A **tailor tack** is one of the oldest methods of marking a pattern, and it is essential to the construction of a garment, especially when using delicate and one-of-a-kind fabrics. I like this method best because it does not leave a hole or a mark on the fabric and it is easy to pull out after you are finished. **The purpose of the tailor tack is to mark the point at which to end the dart.**

Thread your needle with the **contrasting-color thread** and pull it through until you have a double thickness, but do not knot the end. Lay the tracing-paper pattern on top of the fabric. Pin the pattern to the fabric. On the pattern, at the end of the dart line, **where it says "tailor tack," make a tiny stitch** that goes through all three thicknesses (pattern, hankie, and lining). Leave the ends of the thread approximately an inch long, then cut the threads.

Gently remove the pattern, being careful not to pull out the threads from the hankie and lining. Now very slowly separate the hankie and the lining by about a half-inch, being careful to **keep the two fabrics connected by the threads.** Clip the threads between the layers of the fabric, leaving small threads on each piece. Congratulations—you have created your tailor tack! These tiny threads will be pulled out after the dart is sewn.

This section reveals the secrets behind the execution and tailoring of my Hankie Couture dresses. Each description was a lot of fun to write, since the process allowed me to share all the enjoyable details that went into the making of my dresses. I have such a passion for these vintage creations, as you can see by my elaborate descriptions. Enjoy them and feel free to flip back and forth between the pages to take a closer look. After all, Hankie Couture is distinguished by its details. Read them and marvel!

details . . . .

THE MAGIC OF

Hankie Couture®

Hankie Couture Girl *(front cover):* This youthful party dress, made from a lovely patterned hankie sprinkled with pink tulips, is perfect for celebrating the beginning of spring. The scalloped edge follows the petals and leaves of the flowers (see the uncut version on the title page). This dress is one of my favorites! I designed the bodice with a fully scalloped neckline, including the double-layer inset at the front. Each side is different, as the vintage hankie was not symmetrical. The dress back forms a V, and the skirt front is divided into three panels so that I could give an interesting look to the skirt, show off the corners of the hankie, and utilize the entire scalloped edge. The front of the skirt has one panel in the center; to the right and left is the scalloped edge of the hankie and, as you can see, large tulips at each corner. This dress has cap sleeves and a full skirt with matching fuchsia ribbons at the waist. Pearls are nestled in the center of each hand-rolled rose. The matching hatband features pearls dotting a fuchsia satin ribbon. It's so pretty you can almost smell the flowers!

Window Shopper *(page 5):* This marvelous vintage treasure—wonderful for sauntering down the avenue—has thirty-two individual scalloped edges! Each scallop features a flower of a different color. This dress, with its black background—unusual in a vintage hankie— has a full skirt with scallops up the center back seam. The matching scallop-top purse with a gold chain is tacked to the shoulder; the ensemble also includes a parasol and a wide-brim, fully lined matching hat with white piping along the edge, and a red ribbon at the back. Isn't it just the epitome of perfection?

WINE TASTER *(page 12):* A toast: To one of my first inspirational hankie dresses—I will always love and cherish you! This beautiful autumn-hued dress is one of my very first creations. The unusual hankie presented a challenge: I needed to find a solid-color fabric to twin with the awe-inspiring shade of mustard yellow to create contrast against this hankie's deep scalloped edge. The dress has a full skirt with a deep scalloped bodice. The mostly wine-colored hankie also has a back that is just as pretty as the front: the skirt back features saffron-shaded falling leaves and the back of the bodice has two appliquéd leaves sewn to the center. There is a wine-colored rose at the waist. I fashioned a "buttons and bows" hatband that snaps in the back. "Another glass of wine, please."

CALENDAR GIRL *(page 14):* This calendar dress, jacket, and tote will keep any Hankie Couture gal on schedule! The dress features monthly calendars below images of fashion mannequins dancing around the folds of the skirt. I used pure cotton to create the upper part of the skirt and the bodice. The word "August" is appliquéd to the front bodice. The tote bag, in light gray, also has the word "August" on the front and "November" on the back.

The handle on the tote has double rows of contrast stitching. The red coat is also pure cotton, with a contrasting light gray hem and cuffs. She has arrived!

SINGER IN THE RAIN *(page 17):* Need an excuse to go out into the rain and play? This fun raincoat ensemble, which includes a scarf and umbrella, is just the ticket! I designed this double-breasted oversize coat

with set-in sleeves, a round collar, cuffs with hand-rolled lavender trim, and double rows of pink buttons. I sewed the buttons on with contrasting green thread to make it more fun! The coat is fully lined. The hankie's original lavender hand-rolled scalloped edge became the hem of the coat and the edging of the umbrella. The triangular scarf can be snapped under the chin or behind the head. By the way, the purple plastic high heels are completely waterproof!

included is a matching astrological purse (not visible in the photograph), featuring Leo the lion on the front, taken from the original hankie. The tiara is made with pearls and sequins. I am a Leo and I love this outfit for its originality and playfulness.

DUTIFUL DAUGHTER *(page 19):* I used three hankies to create this special embroidered dress, which I designed as a tribute to moms all over the world. The skirt consists of three separate panels, one from each hankie. The front panel, with "Mother"

ROLLER BALLERINA *(page 18):* This is not your typical skating outfit! But for a Leo, it's perfect for getting the crowd's attention. The circular skirt was made from a square vintage handkerchief (shown on page 18). I applied a hand-rolled hem and added red wood buttons in between the "months." The ivory-colored waistband snaps in back. The bra is a halter-style top with gray stripes, taken from the center of the hankie, on the shoulder straps. The bra cups form ties that are knotted in the center. Also

embroidered on it, comes from the first hankie. The embroidered two panels to the right and left, plus the bodice and apron, are cut from the second hankie. The white scalloped edging around the bottom of the skirt and around the apron is from the third hankie. The bodice has faux epaulets. I sewed pearls and tiny royal blue seed beads to the hem, apron, and bodice. A satin ribbon flower with a large pearl center sits at the waist.

HERALD OF SPRING *(page 19):* I created this four-piece ensemble from a single hankie! Note the seam on the center front panel of the skirt: normally, one does not put a seam in the center of the garment—especially the skirt, where it can be seen—but I did this because I wanted large solid sections of white and green to alternate, or "take turns." The green in the center is broken up by a white satin belt with a gold buckle. The model's round hat has a wide green band with a sunflower at the top (not visible in the photograph). The purse has a single sunflower in the front and a green handle. The scalloped hem and umbrella have large white sunflowers along the edges.

CHAPTER 1: THE HANKIE DRESS

PATRON OF THE ARTS *(page 20):* Perfect for the opera or ballet, this circular dress is deserving of a row A box seat. It has thirty-six pink roses and seventy-two white scallops prancing around the bottom of the skirt, which flares out 360°. The fitted bodice has pink satin shoulder straps with three matching pink roses at the top. The waist has two long pink satin bows with matching roses. The skirt is lined in heavy cotton, which adds to its fullness.

The matching wrist corsage provides the perfect finishing touch. Take a bow!

THE IMPRESARIO *(page 22):* Styled in the manner of the 1950s, this shirtwaist dress has a very fitted waist and a full skirt. I cut the bodice and the skirt in such a way that the solid navy color would meet at the waist and the stripes would land at the hem and shoulders. I broke up the color with a fabric self-belt made out of the garland of roses pattern also found on the skirt and bust. I love the way the tiny navy blue stripes are repeated on the sleeves, collar, cuffs, and bodice back. The garland of roses set just above the stripes on the skirt adds a lovely

contrast. I added white pearls to the edge of the blue scallops on the skirt. There are three tiny white buttons on the bodice and the belt is held in place with little loops.

LADY IN BLUE *(page 23):* This sophisticated dress, made from a royal-blue hankie adorned with white flowers, has a petite white scalloped border at the hemline. These scallops are only half an inch apart. I added white pearls to the center of each scallop. The bodice has a deep split in the center with a white scallop on either side. There is a line of tiny white pearl beads that begins just below the bustline and ends at the waist. The edges of the sleeves are also scalloped. I added a white belt and bow to break up all the royal blue and to define the waist. The pillbox-style hat has a scalloped edge at the top with more pearls. The clutch purse has a scallop flap and a small piece of elastic in the back to give our model a better grip.

SUN WORSHIPPER *(page 24):* This delightful dress, whether worn aboard a cruise ship or while walking along sandy beaches, sings the praises of a relaxed excursion. The details start with short sleeves and a square neck (note the shoulder pads). The skirt is emblazoned with vibrant coral stripes and teal, mustard yellow, and fuchsia flowers. The ensemble is completed with a matching purse and a turban-style hat. The belt, purse, and hat feature wooden and plastic colored-bead trim. Hand-rolled roses and piping embellish the turban. There is a low scoop-style back with squared-off edges. Next stop: Rio!

SEASHELL LADY *(page 25):* I loved making this seashell dress! It was strategically cut to highlight all the vertical lines on the vintage hankie. I butted together the edges to create the unusual pattern on the skirt front. The bodice has a slight V neck that is trimmed in white pearls. There is a row of white pearls around the waist, which is accented with three pink seashells. The stripes on the long sleeves line up perfectly with the stripes on the bodice. I sewed rows of pearls at

the upper and lower edges of the hat and attached a seashell to the front. I added pink seashells to the hem of the skirt and I also made a delightful seashell purse with a pearl handle! The vintage shells came from an old necklace of my mom's. I did not hesitate one second to rip this beautiful necklace apart for my Hankie Couture seashell dress! Sorry, Mom!

THE ENTREPRENEUR *(page 26):* It's all in the details! And sometimes, more is better! This vibrant peach and dark navy blue dress was made from a pristine vintage hankie that still had the original tag on. The scallops on this hankie were not symmetrical. The entire neckline from front to back is made with the scalloped edge of the hankie. The front of the bodice is made from five separate pieces, all using the beautiful edges of the hankie set at various angles. The back of the bodice forms a deep V. I added a gold

chain and a pearl with a gold bow to create the belt. The shoulder bag also has a gold chain, pearl, and bow. The model's fitted hat has double rows of gold chains at the top and bottom. The center panel has a scalloped edge in the center. I added white pearls at the tip of each of the scallops. The model is also wearing a pearl necklace and bracelet and a gold necklace with a small rhinestone center! More is better, and it looks so good!

TAXI GIRL *(page 27):* This radiant yellow-and-roses dress is aglow with sunshine! The center of the skirt has a bouquet of roses in the center panel, on either side of which is a scalloped edge. The edges of the sleeves are also scalloped. The bodice has a deep V at the top, ending with four pearl "buttons" at the bottom. There is a thin yellow satin belt at the waist. The hat brim has double rows of scallops dotted with pearls and is trimmed in white tulle with a ruffled edge. The purse has a single-scallop flap with a single white pearl.

WELCOME LADY *(page 28):* This periwinkle blue tea-length dress is the perfect party dress—elegant and comfy! I cut the skirt in such a way as to create a white faux apron in the center. The red roses form the outline of the apron. I added lavender Austrian crystals and pearls in between every scallop on the hem and in between every rose on the apron. The sleeveless bodice has a single deep scallop with a large red rose at the center. The hatband has three flowers at the front, each one embedded with hand-sewn seed beads and a pearl in the center. Lavender crystals travel all around the hatband.

GIRL IN BLOOM *(page 28):* What could be more refreshing for spring than this butter-yellow hankie dress adorned with baby-blue bows? The scoop neckline is framed by a wide collar on which I centered the blue-bow part of the hankie pattern. The skirt consists of five pieces: the three in front are all exactly the same. I added two smaller gussets in between the panels to fill in the hem. The belt, necklace,

and triple-strand bracelet (not visible in the picture) are made from butter-yellow seed beads that are hand-sewn together. There is a yellow rose at the waist, and the hatband has alternating yellow and white roses, each of which has a pearl center.

ORANGE-BLOSSOM GIRL *(page 29):* Clean lines. Elegance. Precision. Tailor-made. That's how I think of this cutting-edge steel-gray dress! The colors are vibrant and really pop! The hem of the skirt and the top of the shoulder bag (not visible in the photograph) sport a double-layer scalloped edge. The dress has a matching single-layer scalloped collar at the bodice that extends around to the back. The wide-brim hat has white piping on the brim and a white bow with a pearl at the back that matches the bow at the waist. The purse has a gold-chain strap.

HOLIDAY HOSTESS *(page 30):* This rich red dress (actually a deep blood red) with white flowers and five separate scalloped skirt panels makes the perfect impression at an at-home holiday get-together. The front panel comes to a V at the hem. Two side panels and two very small gussets connect it all together, providing maximum mileage for the grand white scallop edging. The bodice sports a satin-bow belt with a single white pearl, and the gently scalloped collar adds the finishing touch. Appetizers, anyone?

MISS HOSPITALITY *(page 30):* This delightful dress brings gaiety to a family

gathering or picnic. The details start with the bright white mini-scallops (more than eighty of them) bordering the hem, back of the bodice, and collar. The lush red and white flowers come alive against the mint and hunter-green background. The hatband echoes every color on the dress. It is made with alternating mint green, red, and white flowers with pearl centers. The red flower in the center matches the one at the waist. Our model is wearing a white pearl choker with a red Austrian crystal center and a matching bracelet.

THE DECORATOR *(page 31):* This peaches-and-cream dress makes an arresting impression at any event. Its scallop-edge skirt has bouquets of orange flowers around the center that also cascade down the shoulders and halfway down the sleeves. Double rows of white scallops along the front of the bodice open like petals on either side of the center seam. Short sleeves come to rest just above the elbow. The dress is embellished with seventeen six-pointed rhinestones with pearl centers, including one on each shoe! The model is wearing a small rhinestone belt and necklace. Her scallop-edge hat has a very small layer of netting at the back. Her little pocketbook has a V-shaped flap adorned with scallops and a rhinestone. So sweet!

TRÉS CHIC TRIO *(pages 32–33):* Basically, these three models are all wearing the same style dress, yet each looks very different. All the dresses have full, tea-length skirts, fitted bodices with portrait collars, long bust darts, and three-quarter-length sleeves. The sky-blue dress on the left with the floral cornucopia border has a hand-rolled red edge at the hem and sleeves. There is a red ribbon belt encircling the waist and a small hat with a single red rose in the center. The gray dress in the center with the pink tulips has a scalloped belt and a solid gray collar with white pearl buttons. The sleeves feature a scalloped edge, as does the center back seam. The pure white dress on the right has deep wine-colored cabbage roses all along the hem and sleeves. There is a matching scalloped edge sewn onto the collar. The model is wearing a floral hatband that has four wine-colored roses with pearl centers in front and a bunched-up layer of tulle at the back. There are pearls sewn into each rose on the skirt.

STRAWBERRY GATHERER (page 34): You can practically smell the yummy strawberries on this fun red, white, and blue linen dress! It has a fitted A-line silhouette with vines of strawberries and red flowers in an allover pattern. The bodice has a square neck, front and back, with short cap sleeves and tiny shoulder pads. The matching hat is encircled by a wide red grosgrain ribbon with a large red flower at the back. The matching drawstring purse is very full; the ruffle, which has a hand-rolled edge, is sewn into the shoulder straps. The hem of the skirt and the belt have hand-rolled edges as well. One strawberry iced tea, please!

MADEMOISELLE DE PROVENCE (page 35): This hankie dress almost looks as though it could have been painted by hand! Garlands of pink-and-red flowers travel across the front of the skirt, arrayed against creamy shades of blue. The fitted bodice has a large white cowl-like collar that forms a deep V in the back. The white scallops on the hem are a perfect counterpoint to the white collar. The hat's floppy wide brim can be worn folded back, as shown, or, in sunny weather, the brim can be brought

down to shade the eyes. A red satin ribbon trims the hat, and there is a five-petal flower and a very thin red cord at the waist to add definition to the overall shape.

CHAPTER 2: THE APRON DRESS

ANNIVERSARY MUSE (page 36): One of my personal favorites, this red, blue, and white apron dress features a double-scallop pattern on the skirt and large red roses in the center. The strategically designed skirt features an apron stitched down on the back and bottom, but the front of the apron is free and can lift up. The apron pattern continues around to the back, and the two pieces come together in a perfectly matched seam. The white dress underneath is pure cotton linen. Finishing touches include a matching scallop-rimmed collar, a satin-ribbon belt adorned with a rose, and a floral headband. Many happy returns of the day!

FRATERNAL TWINS (page 38): Being twins at heart means being best friends for life! These girls are wearing nearly identical apron dresses with one small difference: the color! The aprons are splashed with large daisies mixed with small roses in coordinating colors and tiny black polka dots along the scalloped edges. The lavender dress has a double-layer scalloped collar and purple Austrian crystals sewn to the apron. The model wearing it sports a matching necklace and complementary hatband. The bubble-gum-pink dress has a single-layer scalloped collar, pink crystals, and also has a complementary floral hatband. Both girls are wearing satin belts with small flowers at the waist.

BRIDGE PLAYER *(page 39):* You know just by looking at her that this girl is lucky at cards! The sheer apron on this full-skirted, full-length hankie dress features delicately embroidered diamonds, spades, clubs, and hearts. The edge of the apron has red embroidery tracing the miniature scallops, as does the matching collar.

BELLE OF THE BALL *(page 40):* What a vision! There is no question that the woman wearing this full-length, crystal-embellished, hot-pink ball gown is the first to arrive and the last to leave. The bodice on this lovely gown—which features sequins, fuchsia beads, and a sweetheart neckline—falls to slightly below the waist.

The apron has more sequins, a heart-shaped Austrian crystal in the center of the white bow on the bottom of the skirt, and alternating pink and white crystals hanging from the bottom. The matching hat has a self-ruffle with a hand-rolled edge. Underneath the brim are white pearls. I also sewed a row of pink Austrian crystals to the underside of the brim to add interest and sparkle to the model's hair.

PICNICKING LASS *(page 41):* This apron dress is one of my very first creations. I particularly love the unique dress-within-a-dress design: note the enchanting lady pictured on the apron, wearing a full floral skirt, holding an umbrella, and wearing a yellow bonnet! The dress is made from two vintage hankies. The white layer underneath has a thick scalloped edge. There are double rows of this scalloped edge at the back seam of the dress. I sewed pink, blue, and yellow "flowers" to the bottom of the skirt. The center front of the bodice has a small scallop at the waist (from the white hankie) and a full floral scalloped collar. The model is wearing a sheer blue belt with double rows of blue at the top and bottom. The bonnet is fitted with

a double pink-ribbon bow at the back. The full floral scalloped bag has a pink shoulder strap and is lined in white.

SPRINGTIME MAIDEN *(page 42):* I'm in love with the colors of this dress—cinnamon spice and saffron yellow! This was maybe the second dress I ever made and it is a charmer! The model wearing it has plenty of room to kick up her heels in the bias-cut skirt, to which I sewed a row of cinnamon-colored beads along the hem. The huge floral bouquet pictured on the apron is tied with a pink ribbon. The petite collar has a yellow center with a cinnamon edge. I made the belt and hat from fabric flowers and added yellow roses to the center.

ISLAND GIRL *(page 43):* This dress has true Caribbean flava! It's perfect for the queen of the Bermuda Day Parade as she leads a train of mambo dancers behind her float. The full skirt, midriff bodice, and halter straps were made from an all-cotton yellow fabric. The scalloped apron and the twist-front halter top, which is gathered and sewn into the contrasting bodice, were made from a pristine floral hankie. The print features roses, daisies, and blue bows. Baby pearls were sewn to some of the flowers on the apron. A flower shape with a pearl detail decorates the waistline, and the headdress is decorated with a fabric flower and pearls to complete the look. Cha-cha-cha!

QUEEN OF THE CASTLE *(page 44):* The edges on this charming apron dress remind me of the battlements on a castle wall! The colors here work so well, too—deep royal purple and lime green. The ample purple flower on the center of the apron is surrounded by barely there "etchings" of flowers. I added square mirrored beads to the edges. The lavender satin belt has a purple flower in the center adorned with a small white pearl.

GARDEN ENCHANTRESS *(page 45):* Our model is ready to plant flowers for spring! She is wearing a scoop-neck apron dress with cap sleeves and a very full skirt. There are thirty-seven little flowers on her apron alone! The collar is scalloped with nine more flowers. A white satin bow defines the waist. The apron lies over a bright blue checkered gingham fabric.

COTTAGE DWELLER *(page 46):* She merely has to extend her arm and, almost magically, a white dove lands gently on her outstretched hand! This model's long sky-blue dress is simply bursting with vivid flowers in pink, red, and blue. There are hand-sewn roses with white pearls in between every scallop, on the matching hatband, at the waist, and on the band encircling her wrist!

MISTRESS OF PARK PLACE *(page 47):* The occasion? An exhibition at the Textile Faire. Our expert is stunning is her strapless hankie dress and hat. The apron has red opaque beads sewn on the hem; the same beads appear on the front of the bodice and on the blue satin ribbon around the brim of the hat. The upper bodice has a band above the bustline that matches the apron. The very wide-brim hat has a self-ruffle along the edge. The inside is lined in the same black and white checkered print that underlies the apron. The top is covered entirely with fabric from the hankie that comprises the apron. The necklace and bracelet are fashioned from silver, red, and pink beads.

CROCHET PRINCESS *(page 48):* Heavenly and demure, our Crochet Princess looks divine in this dress, with its stunning double-layer white linen apron. At the center of the upper layer is a crocheted medallion with a turquoise flower at the center. Pearls are hand-sewn between every scallop. The bodice has a wide crocheted collar. The subtle cotton dress underneath the apron is a shade lighter than the crochet detail. I designed it this way to make the crochet work appear even brighter.

DAISY SUE *(page 48):* This long floral apron gown is awash with delicate baby blue flowers inside a blue scalloped border. Underneath the apron is a gold-and-white checkered cotton fabric. Note the blue belt and matching hatband. The model is wearing a pearl choker with a blue flower clasp.

CHEF DE CUISINE *(page 49):* It is an auspicious occasion and our model is cooking for fifty. She is a superb cook and she keeps her cool in this light-gray and pink long formal dress. The apron has a hand-rolled edge and an attached polka-dotted belt. The bodice has a wide floral collar and three-quarter-length sleeves. There is a string of medium-size pearls sewn on the lower part of her solid-gray skirt. And she is wearing a special necklace that drapes from her waist and hangs down the center of her skirt! Like the necklace around her neck, it is made from opaque white and dark purple beads. The long chain ends with a large purple crystal that reaches to the center of the pink flower at the bottom of the apron.

CHAPTER 3: THE ACEs

PRESIDENT OF THE WILDFLOWER HERITAGE SOCIETY

(page 50): This very lightweight linen hankie dress features sensational embroidery in a striking floral pattern on the front. It is hard to put a name to the color of this dress—maybe blush, salmon, or the color of a healthy complexion! The light lavender and light teal flowers look like they are growing right from the bottom of the skirt, which has an intricate scalloped edge that's repeated on the bodice. I designed the bodice so that the

two scalloped edges would butt against each other and the solid color would be visible in the middle. The square neckline has a hand-sewn chain with a matching stone at the bottom. There are hand-sewn flowers at the waist that match the hat. The necklace and bracelet match the jeweled embellishment on the bodice.

PROPRIETRESS OF THE TEA ROOM

(page 52): Here, our model wears a mint-green crocheted scoop-neck apron dress with cap sleeves and a floor-length gathered skirt. I found the crocheted sections of this pretty dress at a swap meet, and they were in tatters! I'm not sure what they were part of—perhaps a pillowcase or table runner. In any event, I saw the beauty of the variegated pink crocheted flowers, with their delicate white airy centers, and cut them to fashion the bodice, purse, and hat of this springlike ensemble. I kept the complementary fabric very light, as if to mimic a fresh-cut lawn. Our model carries a crocheted flowered purse (see inset on page 54) that matches the flowers on the dress. The apron features a hand-stitched hem. The hat, which has a wide brim, is turned up to one side and is lined with crochet. One lump or two?

DEAR LITTLE BUTTERCUP

(page 53): This sage-green-and-white classic floor-length apron dress is both elegant and whimsical. It features an embroidered floral bouquet, white pearls, and fabric flowers on the apron, at the waistline, and on the matching hatband. The apron, which overlays a complementary fabric, features a cutwork edge, and the bodice has an embroidered white inset.

THE LINEN SISTERS

(page 54): These elegant linen dresses feature hand-crocheted edges and unique hand-embroidery on the aprons. The model in the blue-and-white dress shows off her apron's busy and intricate design. Her

scoop-neck bodice also has a crocheted collar and a band of embroidery across the bust. There is a black satin bow at the waist. The underlying dress is made from an extra-small gingham print. The strapless dress on the right, on the other hand, features a comparatively small amount of embroidery.

But the scalloped linen apron has white crochet edging and black crochet trim, and the bodice has a matching band of black trim at the top, in the middle of which lies a small rhinestone flower with a black center. The removable belt—which can also be worn as a headband!—has six alternating black and ivory flowers with pearl centers. It snaps in the back.

FAIRY PRINCESS

(page 55): I would sincerely love to be able to wear this alluring and delectable dress. It is at once glamorous and intriguing! The ivory linen has a captivating and colorful cross-stitch design. I added a flange at the bottom of the skirt and double rows of fuchsia

stitching. The sleeves are very full and I made the caps rise well above the neck to make them seem as if they are hugging the model. They taper to just below the elbow. The skirt is extra long, so the model appears to be floating. I'm totally in love with the hat, which was almost as much work as the dress! I joined together the blue blanket-stitched edges of the hankie at the band and crown, then added fuchsia stitching for better definition. The tiny ruffles along the brim of the hat are made from the same blue blanket stitching that runs along the hem of the dress. I added

some fuchsia flowers to the brim of the hat, the front of the skirt, and the bodice.

THE FARMER'S DAUGHTER *(page 56):* This fun and perky dress is so happy! The bodice is very fitted and features a sweetheart neckline. The short skirt has double rows of crochet trim. I added many tiny colorful buttons to both layers of the skirt and the front of the bodice. I embroidered green leaves next to them to make the buttons take on the appearance of flowers!

THE BARISTA *(page 57):* Whoever wears this winsome dress won't have to look very far for refreshment! The heavy white cotton fabric is trimmed everywhere with an equally heavy blue crochet trim—it runs across the front and back of the bodice, the back seam, the hem, and the apron. The large tote bag has an embroidered flower on the front and

more crochet trim on the handle. The hat has a very wide brim with lots of embroidery and more crochet!

THE FOLKSINGER *(page 58):* Our model is captivating in this billowy long black dress with eye-popping embroidered flowers! The uneven fuchsia scalloped hem (part of the original hankie) adds to the drama. The large embroidered collar has a single rhinestone at the center. There are also rhinestones in the center of all the flowers on the skirt. The dress has long, set-in sleeves. The belt and hat are black and fuchsia with rhinestone centers.

THE BALLETOMANE *(page 59):* What better way to show off your love of the dance than with this Swan Lake dress? The powder-blue linen forms a background for the embroidered white swans swimming among the reeds. The fitted bodice features a double row of white scallops accented with white pearls as well as long sleeves tipped with scalloped white edges. The same white scalloped edge trims the hem of the skirt. The model is carrying a small purse with a swan on one side. Her solid-blue hat features a feather, pearls, white netting, and a white bow.

SUNRISE LADY *(page 60):* This pale-yellow linen Rooster dress, and its matching hat and purse, were made from thirteen individual embroidered cocktail napkins, each a tiny four inches square! The sleeveless bodice has a square neck in the front and back. I hand-sewed pearls to every scallop on the white scalloped edges. The strap on the long shoulder bag has a scalloped edge and a single rooster on the front. I added a very thin black belt at the waist to give the dress some definition and break up all the yellow. The circular hat has three roosters on the inside of the brim and tiny white pearls sewn around the edge.

PATCHWORK QUILTER *(page 61):* The apron on this dress was made from two hankies. The hankie with the petit point (extremely small stitches), from which I made the center triangle, was damaged,

but fortunately I was able to salvage the best parts! The rest of the apron is made from a very sheer hankie with pretty little cutouts. I patched the petit point triangle onto the white apron and created narrow piping from the checkered dress around it. The bodice has a very deep V neckline. The petit point at the shoulder is also designed in a V shape to match the neckline and the triangle on the apron. This dress also comes with a very long square shoulder bag decorated with a square patchwork flower (not visible in the photograph). There is a small, wine-colored bow at the waist and a matching floral hatband. A single flower adorns the wristband.

THE FREQUENT FLYER *(pages 62–63):*

This suit is one of my favorite pieces! It was challenging, and I love creating challenges for myself. As with other suits I've made, the slim skirt has front and back darts, a back slit, a waistband, and a snap at the waist. The fitted jacket has a rounded collar and a peplum that flares out at the bottom. The sleeves are three-quarter length. The difficulty lay in the fact that I used the blue blanket-stitched edges as my piping for the

edges of the collar, sleeves, belt, bottom of the jacket, tote bag, and hat! Making this outfit took as much time as any adult ensemble. But I love the results and that's what's important.

LADY OF THE LAKE *(page 64):*

This very long Peacock dress, made from a very small crocheted and embroidered tea towel, is perfect for a lakeside stroll. The peacock takes center stage and is surrounded by bouquets of pastel flowers. The green crochet trim from the tea towel was enough to wrap the brim of the hat three times, and that gave it the extra fullness I wanted. The drawstring clutch (not visible in the photograph) also has a triple layer of crochet trim.

SWEET BLOSSOM DEARIE *(page 65):*

The flowers on this garden-friendly dress are most definitely flourishing—in fact, they are thriving! The sheer apron was made from two layers, one slightly longer than the other. The

flower on the front is repeated on the bodice, where it takes up more than half the surface area. I really love the way the purse came out. It looks alive! I designed the handle so the scalloped edges would form their own unique shape. The hat was made from fabric flowers in coordinating colors; I added pearls to their centers.

SUMMER SWEETHEART *(page 66):*

This pure silk embroidered vintage hankie dress is light as a feather! The skirt, constructed in five pieces, has a pale blue silk blanket-stitched edge. The dress is covered with embroidery in subtle shades of blue, pink, mauve, sage green, and off-white. The bodice has a square neck both in front and in back. The hatband is made from two different-size ribbons—one white and one green—accented with a large pink carnation. A similar pink carnation accents the waist. The birthday card is very old and I thought it went nicely with this vintage ensemble.

GREENHOUSE GIRL *(page 67):*

This pretty model demonstrates what's known as the Greenhouse Effect! Her dress is made from two hankies—one printed, one embroidered. The skirt, made from the printed hankie, has a pretty yellow scalloped edge. I added gold grommets all along the border and bodice. There are two patch pockets on the front of the skirt, one of which has flowers inside. The sleeveless bodice was made from the embroidered hankie, which has gold scalloped edges. The wide-brimmed straw hat is encircled by a green satin ribbon studded with gold grommets.

SUN GODDESS *(page 67):*

Two hankies were involved in the making of this striking dress, with its unique circular skirt. One of them was a full round hankie, pictured to the right of the dress. I used the center of that hankie to create the hat, which is a miniature version of the skirt, mirroring every detail! I added white piping to the brim and a row of turquoise flowers at the front. The bodice, made from the second hankie, is essentially a patchwork design consisting of five layers made from the entire gold scalloped edge of the hankie. The tote bag is made from an embroidered hankie that matched this ensemble beautifully.

CHAPTER 4: SLEEK AND SOPHISTICATED

RAINBOW ROOM GUEST *(page 68)*: This lovely "pure" hankie dress boasts subtle, classic lines. Wear it just for cocktails in town, or for a special dinner. It features a pintucked bodice with contrasting stitching and light gray buttons. The heavenly skirt has a sheer white embroidered inset and dainty white hand-sewn pearls. It embodies haute couture at its finest!

THE CELEBRITY *(page 70)*: Where's my stretch limo? I love the way the specs look with this urbane baby-blue linen five-piece suit, which sports a matching floral cross-stitch sleeveless blouse, a matching purse, and a matching floral cross-stitch wide-brim hat with a self-ruffle. Its slim skirt features welt pockets and a white-piped waistband. The skirt has side slits, and the bolero-style jacket has elbow-length sleeves. All pieces are fully lined. This outfit took as much time to tailor as any adult ensemble I have ever made. With or without sunglasses, this stellar, sophisticated outfit will make you feel like a star!

THE ENTOMOLOGIST *(page 71)*: Our dragonfly expert stays cool in this magical outfit, made from the softest linen I have ever felt. It was a dream to touch and work with. I designed the fitted sleeveless sheath, which snaps in back, to fall just below the knee. The overskirt is removable and has an orange hand-rolled edge. There is a single snap on the waistband. The large floppy hat is trimmed with an orange band. The sheath and hat are lined with soft cotton.

SOCIETY GIRL *(page 72)*: This beautiful three-piece ensemble, perfect to carry any woman from morning to night, has many gold embellishments. The dark navy dress is fitted with an A-line skirt, a square-neck bodice, and a fitted waist. The hat is worn perched to one side, and its brim is turned back and tacked in place. I added flowers, gold beads, pearls, and satin ribbon to the crown. The small purse is lined and gathered below a small gold chain strap. The gold-chain belt overlays a purple satin ribbon at the waist.

THE HORTICULTURALIST *(page 73)*: This violet pansy dress has a fitted A-line style that was popular in the 1940s. The hem has a white scalloped edge with large green flowers. The wonderful green textured fabric-flower belt matches the hem of the skirt and the detail on the yoke and sleeves. The hat has feathers, pearls, white roses, and ribbon. The purse is circular and has a scalloped edge. The shoulder strap also has a scalloped edge and forms a bow at the shoulder. There are three tiny white pearls at the purse front. The original uncut hankie appears on the right side of the page. Don't forget to smell the flowers!

THE JET-SETTER *(page 74):* Our Hankie Couture girl wants to be noticed, and that's why she is wearing this red linen five-piece suit! The skirt, jacket, and hat were made from a single red hankie with a white hand-rolled edge. The blouse, which snaps in the back, was made from a white hankie embroidered with red and pink flowers. All the pieces are fully lined. The slim skirt has a narrow waistband that closes with a single snap. The swing-style hip-length jacket is cut most fully at the bottom. It features two patch pockets and three-quarter-length sleeves. I used the white hand-rolled edge from the red hankie as the trim, or piping, for all the pieces. I cut out a flower from the blouse and appliquéd it to the hat. The little purse is a combination of the two hankies: the body of the purse is from the red hankie; the flap is from the embroidered hankie. The purse has a long gold chain strap.

DEPARTMENT STORE BUYER *(page 75):* I wanted to use a different strategy in creating a dress from this sweet little hankie, which I found to be so dainty and graceful. I used the light green border as trim for the shoulders, belt, hat, and purse. The sleeves are gathered into the yoke of the deep V neckline (in front and back). I formed little darts at the bust and held them in place with a gold bead. The hat crown is all flowers; the band is made from the center part of the hankie and the green border. The little purse also has a green pointed flap and a gold chain.

THE WORLD TRAVELERS *(pages 76–77):* Diversity was the motivating factor behind this pair of lovely girls! I wanted two different looks based on

one sophisticated silhouette. Both slim skirts have front and back darts, back slits, a waistband, and a snap at the waist. The fitted jackets have a peplum that flares out at the bottom. The sleeves are three-quarter length. Both jackets have a rounded collar, and all the pieces are lined. The white linen suit on the left features embroidered flowers, crochet trim, and open stitchwork. The sleeves have turned-back pointed cuffs dotted with white pearls. The hat, which fits snugly on the head, rises up higher in the front and sits lower in the back. The band at the bottom comes from the same hankie, as does the purse our traveler holds in her hand. For the suit on the right, I attached a separate scalloped band (from the same hankie, of course!) to the hem of the bright blue floral skirt; in a unique detail, the scallops lie at the top of the band, not the bottom. The edge of the jacket peplum is also scalloped, as are the sleeves on the jacket. The wide-brim hat has a strand of pearls around the crown and a large white flower and bow at the back. The purse has a white beaded handle and a small white pearl at the flap. I added a small piece of elastic in the back so the model could "grip" her purse more securely!

OPERA AFICIONADO *(pages 78–79):* This hankie was a great find because it was so big! Most hankies are approximately twelve to thirteen inches square. This one was eighteen inches! Its size allowed me to create a very full skirt, just a little shy of a complete circle, and a matching long-sleeve jacket. The bodice cuts straight across the bustline and is anchored in place with thin black shoulder straps. The cropped jacket has a contrasting wide black collar and cuffs. Both the collar and the cuffs use the white hand-rolled edge of the hankie as trim. There are two little faux "button" pearls on each side of the jacket opening. I made the hat very small, with a little brim trimmed in white pearls. The purse is also trimmed in black.

CHAIRWOMAN OF THE SUPPER CLUB *(page 81):* The hankie for this dress came from Boston, and the hankie for the accompanying jacket came from California, my home state. I was bowled over when I put them together, and dropped everything to create this dressy suit. First I cut the skirt on the bias to capture the lovely ribbon bow just at the front. The entire scalloped hem had to be pieced on to the edge of the skirt, yet it all looks like one piece! What fun! Then I centered the front of the bodice on the flowers, and added white trim to the very top of the shoulders for contrast. The belt is a thick braid in light gray. The purse has a scalloped flap trimmed in the same gray braid. The back of the mid-calf-length jacket is where the interest lies! I let the long edges of the scallops "kiss," and the pretty pattern you see is the result. The hems of the sleeves are scalloped, the collar is very wide, and white bows sit atop each of the shoulders. There is a small patch pocket on the right side with a tiny hankie peeking out! The asymmetrical hat has beaded trim in shades of gray and a white ribbon encircling the crown.

THE SOPHISTICATE *(page 82):* It's no wonder that this model stops traffic! She is a walking vision in her sage-green border-print ensemble. I used the black-and-white sections of the hankie to create her wonderful belt and ruffled hat. I outlined the belt with two rows of gold chain, and then I added a third belt, in pearl and gold, just below the waist! Perfect! The little handbag is also embellished with gold and pearls (my mom always told me that more is better). The hat is the real charmer, with its frilly ruffle and strand of pearls and gold going around the crown.

CAREER GIRL *(page 83):* Business attire never looked so good! This gal is ready to put in a long day at work, then go out for dinner and cocktails in this ultra-slim pencil dress. The empire waist is marked by a navy-and-white polka-dot band just below the bust. The strategically cut bodice places the same polka-dot pattern at the top, forming a faux collar, which continues around the back. The three-quarter-length sleeves were strategically cut so they end with navy blue. There is a little polka-dot pocket on the right hip large enough for a small hankie, just in case! The hat is fitted with red floral accents.

CHAPTER 5: JUST FOR FUN!

LAB TECHNICIAN *(page 84):* This model is a "body of knowledge," arriving in her Chemistry dress just in time to impart a bit of wisdom in her typically logical and methodical way! The long full skirt of this fun dress has a thick obi-style sash. I fitted the upper part of the bodice, front and back, with a small flange to strategically capture the circles in the hankie pattern across the bust. (A flange is created by making a small fold in the fabric, then stitching a quarter-inch away from the fold.) The purse and belt feature the same circles. I hand-beaded the headband by threading matching wooden beads onto a very narrow piece of elastic. Our chemist is happy in the lab among the beakers, atoms, Bunsen burners, and microscopes!

THE CRYING GIRLS *(page 86):* Sympathy loves company in these Crying Hankies outfits. The aprons and bib-style square-neck collars, as well as the matching "message" tote

bags, were all made from a single hankie. I used a complementary mini-gingham fabric to set off the boldness of the aprons and collars, which have hand-rolled red edges. Everyone agrees—"There are too many taxes and not enough hankies!"

THE ORGAN GRINDER *(page 87):* I wish I had a dollar for every time I said, "I must have that little hankie!" I remember saying those exact words when I saw the adorable hankie from which I made this unique dress. Wow! Such a cute little imp. There are very unusual colors at work here: light pink, salmon, dark orange, and lime green! I used accents of the rolled lime-green edge along the wide cuffs of the sleeves, the frilly collar, and the belt. I fashioned a hat with the monkey sitting playfully at the top! I was able to squeeze out a tiny parasol, too.

THE BREAKFAST ALLIANCE CLUB *(pages 88–89):* These "accountability" outfits ensure that our club members have fun while keeping focused on their goals. The Vitamins/Calorie dress illustrates the nutritional and caloric content of various foods. It features princess seaming with two inverted pleats on each side of the skirt. The coordinating mandarin-style coat has "Vitamins" and "Calorie" appliquéd on the front, back, and both sleeves. The body of the coat is new, 100 percent cotton. I thought the little

squares on the print complemented the hankie very nicely. The pillbox-style hat and small purse carry the calorie message, too. They and the dress are all made from the same handkerchief (shown at the top of page 82). The Keep Slim dress is a tailored "pure" hankie dress that illustrates various exercise techniques, has a fitted waist with a green ribbon belt, pearl buttons, bust darts, a round collar with green piping made from the hand-rolled edge of the hankie (shown at the bottom of page 82), and short sleeves with shoulder pads. The dress hem, hat, and tote bag also have hand-rolled green edging.

BIRTHDAY GIRL *(page 90):* This elegant red apron dress, with a birthday wish inscribed, features a complementary polka-dotted fabric paired with the original hankie. Note the scalloped border with white daisies on the apron edge, the square neckline, and the very full train-back skirt (the train is not visible in the photograph). This dress is lined in pure cotton. It has a V back (not visible in the photograph),

a rhinestone waistband, and a fancy matching wide-brimmed hat—trimmed with lace, tulle, hand-rolled roses, pearls, and a feather. Imagine sweeping into the room in this confection!

MESSENGER OF THE HEART *(page 91):* A romantic fantasy, this lovely dress has an apron made from three separate hearts sewn together. I embellished all the hearts with roses and rhinestones. The fitted scoop-neck bodice has a very long V-shaped collar. The white-and-red polka-dotted dress underneath has a blind-stitched hem. The hatband is studded with pearls.

FEARLESS EXPLORER *(page 93):* It matters not where the sailing expedition takes our Hankie Couture girl: what matters is that she arrives there in style, wearing her Bon Voyage strapless dress! I used every single bit of hankie for this ensemble—there wasn't

a scrap left over. The Bon Voyage border was sewn separately onto the bottom of the skirt, and I used the turquoise hand-rolled edge as piping along the seam of the bodice. The playful hat shows everyone that this is one fun gal! She is ready to gallivant on the high seas for months at a time, since she carries plenty of custom-made matching luggage with her, including two cruise ship tote bags.

THE COMEDIENNE *(page 94):* I love a nice normal life with just a touch of the bizarre thrown in for good measure—and this dress fits in with the bizarre part! It's made from a very old silk hankie that I found at a swap meet! I fashioned the bodice into a bra-style top, then gave it a twist in the center to create fullness. The backless design features two straps that snap at the nape of the neck. The skirt is very long and full because I wanted as many faces as possible here. The tote bag has two handles and a row of yellow beads sewn at the top. The hat is a hoot, with two ladies' faces perched on the crown! There are rows of yellow beads at the top and bottom of the hat. There is a single row of beads at the waist.

FRIEND TO THE SQUIRRELS *(page 95):* No, our model is not eccentric; she just loves to nurture furry little animals, especially squirrels! I had fun embellishing this Squirrel dress with a bracelet that I'd had since I was a little girl. I had no qualms about ripping it apart. The colorful stones looked like they could be food for the squirrels! The green piping at the edge of the skirt was cut out and sewn on separately, and I added a false hem. The purse is square and shows a green squirrel on

the front and a tan squirrel on the back. The band of the hat is adorned with several colored stones and shows a rust-colored squirrel eating a nut!

THE ORNITHOLOGIST *(page 96):* This delightful old hankie was in a very sad state of ruin. It was threadbare and had more than a few holes. A small piece had been torn off. Many of the poor birds had "peep holes" on their little bodies! But it was so cute and I just had to have it, regardless of its condition. The first thing I did was to cut white cotton fabric into little squares and place one piece behind every bird. This added strength and made the colors pop. Next, I took two strands of black embroidery floss and outlined each and every bird with even little stitches. I also added these stitches to the hem, belt, upper bodice, and the fabric bow at the waist. I even managed to salvage enough fabric to make a matching tote bag, on the front of which I embroidered the words "Bird Seed."

THE DOG WALKERS *(page 97):* I love dogs! Even though I no longer have my precious Coco, I'm always on the lookout for any object that depicts man's best friend. The poodle hankie that I made into the dress on the left was a great find (and very expensive). I cut

the skirt in a way that allowed me to make the most of the asymmetrical lines of the design. Our model is really cinched in at the waist with a jet-black cotton ribbon. I repeated this black outline on the hat. I also cut out one of the extra dogs and appliquéd it to the front of the shoulder bag. I added the white pearls just for fun! The Scottie dress, on the right, is made from two hankies. The doggie hankie was extremely small, so I was delighted when I came across the hankie embroidered in gold and chocolate brown that I used for the bodice, as the colors were a perfect match! I created a long, tapered V inset at the front of the bodice to showcase the brown "paw prints." I used the gold scalloped edge of the hankie as a contrasting border along the entire edge, even on the back. The neckline is square in front, but tapers to a V in back. I crocheted a brown belt and added a "dog bone" button at the waist. The headband has an extra doggie bone in case someone gets hungry! Woof, woof!

THE PERFECT WIFE *(page 98–99):* She is the envy of the neighborhood, this girl! Wherever she goes, women ask her for her sage advice! I wanted the "How to Keep Your Husband" border to be outlined, so I used the red hand-rolled edging of the hankie to highlight these words. I pieced together the bodice because I wanted to get the couple kissing on the front. I added little square gold grommets at the intersecting navy blue lines. The skinny purse has a picture of the model's "husband" and Cupid on the front!

TUTTI FRUTTI WOMAN *(page 101):* Our model remains cool and delicious in this halter-top linen dress, perfect for a hot summer night. I turned up the white hand-rolled edge of the skirt to create an interesting white horizontal line. The twisty bra-style top has white shoulder straps and a white midriff. I placed the ruffle encircling the hat at the top, so the hat would mimic a cup filled with natural fruit. And I added plastic fruit to the hat, bodice, and hem of the skirt just for fun!

CHAPTER 6: SPECIAL OCCASIONS

NIGHT OWLS *(page 102):* When in doubt, always wear black and white. It guarantees that you will always look good. The black-and-white apron dress on the left was made from two hankies sewn together in alternating layers from top to bottom. The little white hankie has the cutest itsy-bitsy

embroidered flowers in black and white, while the solid black hankie has a wide mesh border, also in black and white. This dress is very detailed! I added an antique beaded necklace to the apron and bodice. The hatband consists of a row of pearls on top of a black-and-white ribbon. The model's little black satin belt has tiny loops on each side. The strapless dress on the right, embellished with a diminutive white jewel-like embroidered design, features a five-panel skirt. I used three corners of the hankie to accent the front and back of the skirt and the last corner to accent the front of the bodice. Then I further embellished the skirt and waistline with bows made of white satin ribbon and pearls. I sewed fifteen of these ribbon-and-pearl bows tightly together to make the headband!

STARS ON THE RED CARPET *(page 104):* Three cheers for red, white, and blue! These dresses take patriotic colors to a new level! The short dress, on the left, was made from three separate hankies—one red, one white, and one blue. The skirt consists of six layers—two for each color. The layers get shorter as they travel up from hem to waist. The bodice is fitted with thin satin shoulder straps. I embellished the waist and bodice with white and red roses and added large ribbon bows to the waist. This dress is light as a feather. The dress on the right was made from two hankies. I knew the moment I saw the hankie with the tiny red flowers that I would be taking it home! Some time later, I found the hankie with the larger red flowers and I knew instantly that these hankies would marry each other! The bottom layer of the skirt is cut with the grain; the remaining three layers are cut on the bias. For the bodice, I butted the edges of the little hankie together, leaving a small white space in the middle for contrast. There are tiny red rhinestones on the skirt and a large flower at the waist, and the model is holding her floral-and-rhinestone hatband above her head. Ta-da!

THE PARK PRESERVATIONIST *(page 106):* It is amazing how our model can look so

beautiful and sexy, yet all we really see are her hands! This elaborate floral and polka-dot dress has long two-piece "muttonchop" sleeves. The upper parts are very full and gathered into the narrow, fitted parts below the elbow. I added many pearls to the dress as well as the sheer baby-blue belt. I loved making the hat, which features multicolored roses with pearls sewn in the centers. I looped long strands of pearls around the brim, the edge of which is trimmed in white piping.

MISS KENTUCKY DERBY *(page 106):* This lovely floral dress, made from a heavily machine-embroidered hankie, has a very full and long skirt. I created a flange near the edge of the apron and embroidered it with a blue running stitch, then added pearls to the entire ensemble. The bodice has a sweetheart neckline. The floppy hat has a ruffle made from the blue edge of the hankie. I also used the edge of the hankie as trim for the top of the tote bag.

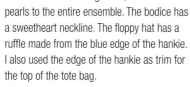

BEARER OF GOOD TIDINGS *(page 107):* Wouldn't it be just too much fun to wear this dress—a long column-style sheath that ends at mid-calf—in real life? I cut the embroidery part of the dress on the bias, but I cut the lining with the grain so the dress would not stretch out. I added clear sequins and seed beads to the centers of the flowers. The flowers on the wrist corsage are sewn to a white ribbon.

SHARI, THE BRIDE *(page 108, bottom; page 109; and page 112, far left):* May the woman who catches the bride's bouquet dream of walking down the aisle in this billowy white cutout princess dress. The lace-effect handkerchief from which it's made is lined with two layers of the softest shade of pink chiffon I could find. The glorious chiffon feels so wonderful, and I wanted to give the dress a little visual contrast, something different from the traditional white. The full skirt has a train in back, and the overall

blossoming effect includes puffy half-sleeves. The fitted sweetheart neckline has princess seaming, and I decorated the entire dress with pearls and sequins. The headpiece is made from white fabric flowers, white ribbons, and pearls, and tapers to a V in back. The bouquet is fitted with a bit of elastic so the model can "hold" it properly. I do take this dress to be my one and only wedding gown, to love and cherish now and forever!

IDA, THE SISTER OF THE BRIDE *(page 108, far left; and page 112, center):* This strapless dress, made from a small machine-embroidered vintage tablecloth, has a fitted bodice, a full skirt, and a glorious array of large flowers in several shades of pink. A fuchsia ribbon encircles the model's waist.

MARSHA, THE MAID OF HONOR *(page 108, bottom right; page 110; and page 112, right):* This intricate machine-embroidered dress, made from the same small vintage tablecloth as the bride's sister's dress, honors the bride with a cornucopia

of colors that complement the sheer pink lining of the bride's dress. This dress has a square neckline in front and back, cap sleeves that are part of the close-fitting bodice, and a very full skirt with a long train. I embellished the entire dress with sequins and pearls. The model is wearing a floral headband with flowers that match the blooms on the front of the skirt. A fuchsia ribbon encircles her waist.

ISABEL, A DEAR FRIEND OF THE BRIDE *(page 108, top center; and page 113, left):* This dress was made from a large vintage placemat! I designed the skirt in layers, so that the center front would fall to the knees, the sides would

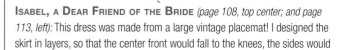

gradually taper downward, and the back would fall to the floor. The bodice features a lacy front overlay, and there is a matching long bow at the waist.

ROSE, A BRIDESMAID *(page 108, top right; page 111; and page 113, right):* Every bridesmaid wants to look spectacular. She wants a dress that doesn't scream "bridesmaid!" and she wants to be able to

wear her dress to other venues after the wedding. This fun strapless ivory sheer lace gown fits the bill perfectly. It has a triple-tier eyelet skirt, each layer more full than the last. It practically dances on its own! The bodice has a matching scalloped band and a matching ivory satin bow at the waist. The large matching shoulder bag—perfect for carrying flowers—is more like a soft basket, as it is open at both ends.

THE DIVA *(pages 114–115):* I have never seen anything like the tiny hankie from which I made this dress! As soon as I first laid eyes on it, I was smitten. My dilemma was that it was so small, only ten inches wide. Eventually, in my travels, I ran across a solid white linen hankie with a variegated crocheted edge and clear sequins (look for them on the ruffles) and I knew I found the mate for my concert hankie! I made the skirt as long as possible to capture the full

musical scene, especially the people in the balcony. The white hankie served two purposes—first as a lining and also as a bustle in the back of the skirt, for which the crocheted edging was especially useful. The corset-style blouse, a separate piece, features the crocheted edge of the white hankie along the deep scoop neckline and also at the peplumed bottom. The blouse snaps in front. The gloves are made from the concert hankie, to which I added the

other hankie's crochet trim at the wrist. The earrings were made from some real marcasite earrings of my own that I cut into a triangle shape.

TWIRLY GIRL *(pages 116–117):* There is perpetual motion in my fun dance dress! The fully lined full-circle skirt was made from the hankie shown on page 108. The embroidered strapless bodice, cut from another hankie, is a perfect match. Doesn't the dress look spectacular as it twirls on the dance floor?

THE DEBUTANTE *(page 118):* Purple is my favorite color. No white dress with satin gloves for me! This spectacular strapless apron-style gown, which features a floor-length skirt that trails slightly longer in back, has a dropped waist and is form-fitted with eight darts. The skirt is decorated with large cabbage roses and a double-scallop edge. Here, the apron overlays a complementary fabric. Notice the matching scalloped bodice band and floral hat. I'll need to practice my curtsy.

THE STARGAZER *(page 119):* This very sheer lavender nylon scalloped dress with sequins conjures up clouds and lightness, and feels perfect for dancing. I love these rare nylon hankies; to me, they have a magical, fairy-tale look to them. Dark purple touches dot the inside of each tiny scallop— and there are more than a hundred scallops on this dress alone! The five panels in the skirt, the round scallop collar, the matching floral hatband, and the hand-sewn sequins applied to all the scalloped edges heighten the ethereal effect. Let the music and the festivities begin!

CHAPTER 7: SLEEPWEAR

PINK LADY *(pages 120–121):* This sexy (unlined!) nightgown, made from a pale pink hankie, features an open-weave design and tatted lace. Falling to mid-calf, and styled with an A-line silhouette, it also features a long, lacy V-shaped collar that looks somewhat like a bib. The back of this gown was strategically cut so that each of the model's legs would show through the openwork. I pressed the seams to the outside to form a double edge along the entire back seam. I did this not only to showcase the beautiful edges of the hankie but also to add coverage to the derrière! One must always practice discretion!

MORNING PERSON *(page 122):* There is nothing more comfortable than a favorite peignoir and slippers, and our model looks so cozy and comfy in this very, very full mid-calf dressing gown, which has a lined yoke and full sleeves gathered to form a self-ruffle. I cut out two daisies and carefully stitched them to her little slippers to keep her feet warm! I also added a very long white satin ribbon to the top of the gown. I usually keep these ribbons narrow, about ⅛-inch wide, but this ¼-inch ribbon gives the gown a more comfy look than the thinner ribbon. The vintage hankie from which I fashioned this peignoir is of exceptionally high quality—they just don't make them like this anymore. All four corners have mitered edges (joined angularly at the seam). Also, the entire embroidered edge is lined! If you can find such a hankie in your travels, snap it up!

BEAUTIFUL DREAMER *(page 123):* It's hot outside, but this little two-piece baby

doll jammy set keeps our model cool all night long! The short shorts have an elastic waistband. The top is full and styled with a narrow, fitted yoke. I very carefully cut out six of the fuchsia flowers from the hankie and hand-sewed them to the yoke. I used the straight edge of the hankie for the hem of the jammy top and the shorts legs. The little white buttons are stitched on with matching pink thread, and the model is wearing a pink ankle corsage.

THE EARLY RISER *(page 124):* It's hard to sleep when these cute jammies are so much fun to wear. And what fun they were to create! I made the cropped camisole from the embroidered portion of the original hankie, shown at the top of page 112, and added lace straps. To the pull-on pants, which have an elastic waistband, I added pink bows with pearls just below each knee. I also added lace at the bottom of the cami and pants. This outfit is semi-sheer—peekaboo!

SLEEPING BEAUTY *(page 125):* This sophisticated two-piece pajama set features a slightly oversized shirt-style top with a stand-up collar, three-quarter-length sleeves, and four tiny pink buttons with snaps underneath. The cropped pants have an elastic waistband. There is a hand-rolled hem at the bottom of each leg, the top, and the sleeves. The pink scalloped border print is divine!

SLUMBER PARTYERS *(pages 126–127):* These four nightgowns are all designed in the same style—cut just above the knee, with round necks and shoulder snaps—yet I wanted to make each one look distinctive. The white nightie on the left, decorated with tiny fuchsia flowers, has scalloped edges that meet at the waistline. I sewed white pearls in the center section and added hand-stitching to the hem. I also sewed pearls in the shape of a flower at the shoulders. The model holds a white hankie pillow with a pink crocheted edge. The model next to her wears a powder-blue gown with a double row of daisies centered at the bust. I carefully cut out another twelve daisies from the hankie and hand-appliquéd them to the hem. I fastened yellow beads at the shoulders. The very sheer white gown at the center right features

asymmetrical bias-cut front and back panels—three in the front and four in the back. I cut the hankie this way to be able to capture the large bouquet of yellow daisies tied with a blue bow at the front. There are also daisies sewn at each shoulder, and the model is holding a ruffled-edge hankie pillow. For the light-blue gown at the far right, I made a double row of scallops by having the pink edges of the hankie meet closely in the center (they are barely ¼ inch apart). Then I added white pearls in between each small scallop. Pink roses rest on the shoulders, and the model is holding an embroidered pale blue hankie pillow with a crocheted, gathered edge.

COMPASSIONATE FRIEND *(page 128):* Not only is our model wearing her heart on her sleeve, she's wearing it on her pants as well! I was overjoyed to find the beautiful hearts-and-roses hankie from which these jammies were made. It was in mint condition, and still had the original tag! I fashioned the top with three-quarter-length sleeves, a three-piece back, and a foldover pointed collar that can be worn up or down. I cut the pant legs longer at the outsides of the ankles than I did at the inseam. Then I added small pieces of hankie to the inner legs to rebalance the hemline.

THE DAYDREAMER *(page 129):* A little glamour goes a long way on this cute two-piece crop-top pajama set! The square-neck top, which snaps in the back, and the pant legs each have green

seed beads sewn to the bottom. The pants have an elastic waistband.

LADY OF LEISURE *(page 130):* The hankie from which this outfit was made practically jumped out and forced itself on me when I first saw it! I totally loved the delicious flowers along the border and the sky-blue center! I made the tiny ruffles by cutting out the edges of the hankie and gathering them at the top and bottom of the bustier and the brim of the puffy nightcap. The long rows of pearls down the center of the bustier are for looks only: there are snaps underneath. I sewed a long floral inset into each pant leg, so that each leg consists of three pieces. The daybed that our model rests on consists of four different embroidered or crocheted pieces. The cushions feature embroidered floral garlands topped by delightful blue bows (not visible in the photograph). The lower edge of the bottom cushion is pieced with blue crochet trim and more embroidery stitches. The arms of the bed and the cushion inset were made from a vintage tablecloth. The bed skirt was made from a vintage crocheted piece. I added pleats to all four corners. The back of the daybed has a white crocheted medallion, not visible in the photograph.

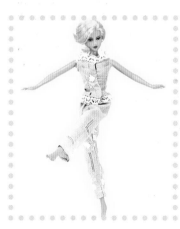

YOGA LADY *(page 131):* The delicate baby-blue hankie from which these pajamas were made has so many beautiful details, all done in white—white appliqué flowers, bits of white embroidery, white cutwork that allows the skin to show through. Good-looking and comfortable, it's the perfect outfit for a good night's sleep. I added white lace to the top and bottom of the fitted bustier, but did not add any buttons because I felt they were a visual distraction. The bustier snaps in front, and the neckline can be folded down so the top can be worn off the shoulder if desired. The ankle-length pants have an easy elastic waistband.

THE HEIRESS *(page 132):* I'm partial to purple and I had a blast decorating this gown to the point of excess! I started adding pearls, sequins, and bugle beads to all the flowers printed on the hankie, and every time I came into my sewing room, I added more . . . and more . . . and more! The double-breasted fitted bodice of the robe features two small purple buttons. Princess seams are sewn into the very full A-line skirt. I embroidered a thin purple belt at the waist to break up the mass of white. I also designed the robe so that the flowers would appear to be growing up the sides. The sleeves have a scalloped edge, and more beading at the cuffs. The extremely short fitted teddy accentuates our model's long, lean legs! I placed the scalloped edges of the hankie at the top of the bodice front and at the bottom of the legs, and beaded those areas, too!

ROSE OF WASHINGTON SQUARE *(page 133):* Strategy plays a big part in the design of this empire-waist, below-the-knee nightgown. I pressed the hankie's embroidered edges to the outside along the length of the entire front seam so that our model's body is barely camouflaged! The two scallops strategically placed at the top of the bustline overlap the scallop-edge shoulder straps and create a heart shape at the center of the bust area. Note that the scallops on the shoulder straps face out, toward the arms. I hand-beaded the white necklace and placed a red flower in the center, then gave our model a small coordinating wrist corsage.

NIGHTTIME STORYTELLERS *(pages 134–135):* I'm proud to say that the lovely appliquéd tea towel from which this nightgown was made used to belong to my mom. I'm so happy to be able to use it for my book! It features a most unusual appliqué: the back of a woman wearing a pale-blue floor-length nightgown and carrying a green-and-white striped hatbox. Note the tips of her slippers peeking out from under the nightgown! We can also see the suggestion of her legs beneath the gown. Oh, yes—her derrière is actually made from two covered buttons! I made the long-sleeve

A-line robe from the same tea towel, and added two patch pockets and a belt. Then I machine-embroidered all the edges on both pieces in a scallop stitch in the exact same shade as the tea towel. This gives the gown and robe a rich yet subtle elegance.

SLEEPY GIRL *(page 135):* The cute old-fashioned girl embroidered on this white linen hankie has a long yellow braid, a lantern, and, um, rather prominent breasts! These noticeable appendages are actually made from little covered buttons. I added a small piece of vintage lace to the hem, sleeves, and neckline of the figure's red nightgown and fashioned an old-style sleeping cap with lace and red ribbons to match the design of the appliqué.

ANGEL OF THE MORNING *(page 136):* What a perfect way to start off the morning—or end a long day! The top on this two-piece baby-doll

set features rows of daisies along the narrow yoke, the front, and the bottom. I carefully cut out the daisies from the hankie and sewed them on one at a time. The top snaps in back. The pants have a comfortable elastic waistband. Of course, the model is also wearing what every woman should wear to bed—pearls! She has them around her neck, around her wrist, and on the ribbon that she wears as a headband.

LADIES OF LUXURY *(pages 136–137):* These embroidered diaphanous negligees have the same style of overlapping bodice, but one skirt is ankle-length and the other falls above the knee. For the long gown, at the left, I created a two-layer asymmetrical border at the bottom, then added a row

of shiny matching bugle beads at the hem and at the empire waist. For the short gown, on the right, I sewed the edges of the foldover flap at the bodice wrong-sides-together to create the small seams along the entire front of the gown. Our model stays under the covers because her gown is very sheer!

GODDESS OF SLUMBER *(page 138):* Sophisticated. Sexy. Demure. Ravishing. These are just some of the adjectives that describe this mid-calf-length ivory lace nightgown. The empire-waist bodice is covered with the same lace that adorns the bottom of the gown. The solid part of the gown ends well above the knees; the deep lacy border, well below. The back is totally lacy, and not lined. The ivory rose at the waist sits atop a matching ivory bow. I gave our model a wrist corsage for added romance.

CONFETTI THROWER *(page 139):* I loved the confetti print on this hankie and I was excited to use it to create this beautiful two-piece ensemble! The top has three-quarter-length sleeves, a notched collar, patch pockets, and tiny pink buttons sewn on with white thread for contrast. I used the scalloped edges of the hankie to trim the pockets, sleeves, pant legs, and the hem of the shirt-style top. The jammy bottoms have a stretchy elastic waistband.

acknowledgments . . . .

THE FRIENDS OF

Hankie Couture®

I must first thank my husband, Brian, for being there for me every step of the way. Without him, this book would not have come to fruition. He has always believed in me and my talents. He has been my backbone. His steadfastness in keeping the smallest details on track kept everything moving along smoothly. I cannot count the times, after he spent a long day at work, that he would come home and devote his attention to Hankie Couture, his "second job." He never complained; he was never "too tired." He never ran out of patience. I could cry just thinking about it. Thank you, Brian, from the bottom of my heart and soul.

I also owe heartfelt thanks the producer of my original self-published book, Liz Walker. Our fortuitous meeting in Brimfield, Massachusetts, where I was antiquing with Brian, was a lucky day indeed! Liz went above and beyond the call of duty in each and every instance. She devoted herself to making this the best book possible. Her keen eye was continually focused on the minutest detail. She made herself available to talk even in the wee hours of the morning. Liz is a woman of impeccable ethics and high standards. Her determination and perseverance made it the most special and beautiful book in the whole world!

Our Graphic designer, Joy Chu . . . Simply put, she is a creative genius! Joy's artistic spirit breathed life into my Hankie Couture dresses, dolls, and the entire book. One of my fondest memories is watching Joy assemble the dolls in the photo tent, enriching each scene with her innovative, inspired styling. But these photo sessions were only half the story. Joy then created the pages, one by one, using her original, fertile imagination to make them truly magical. She is a one-of-a-kind original!

My original book editor, Barbara Clark . . . My hat goes off to this incredibly savvy woman, who allowed me to use all my own words and then made them better. Talk about a keen eye! Nothing got past this woman! Every period, every comma, every sentence, and all their interrelations were dissected and put in their proper order. She constantly amazed me.

Bryan McCay, our photographer, is a true professional with a down-to-earth personality and a very creative eye. His caring shows through in each and every picture. He was able to capture on film all the love that went into the making of my doll dresses. Our photo shoots were a blast, especially since Bryan provided the wonderful music that played in the background while we worked!

Another thank you goes out to Bill and Sherry Simonic, the proprietors of the Yankee Cricket Bed & Breakfast in Brimfield, my home away from home. This is where it all began—my first trip to Brimfield and my first meeting with Liz. Bill and Sherry showered Brian and me with love and kindness even before they knew who we were. Brian and I can't wait to go "home" for another visit!

Working with my editor, Cindy De La Hoz, on this new edition of my book was a total pleasure: all mine!! She was so professional and her excitement showed through with every email and phone conversation. What fun it is to have you in my world!

Corinda Corinda!! My designer, Corinda Cook, threaded the needle with her bull's eye, spot-on cover design! One cannot improve on perfection. It is perfect in every way: unequaled and out of this world!!

Our publisher, Chris Navratil: Thank you for always loving my book! Thank you for publishing my book! Thank you for being part of the Hankie Couture world!